Youth and Development in Cuba

Richard N. Gioioso ·
Zaily Leticia Velázquez Martínez ·
Carlos Manuel Osorio García
Editors

Youth and Development in Cuba

palgrave
macmillan

Editors
Richard N. Gioioso
Saint Joseph's University
Philadelphia, PA, USA

Zaily Leticia Velázquez Martínez
Universidad de Holguín
Holguín, Cuba

Carlos Manuel Osorio García
Universidad de Holguín
Holguín, Cuba

ISBN 978-3-030-90865-2 ISBN 978-3-030-90866-9 (eBook)
https://doi.org/10.1007/978-3-030-90866-9

This Palgrave Macmillan imprint is published by the registered company Springer Nature Switzerland AG
The registered company address is: Gewerbestrasse 11, 6330 Cham, Switzerland

Contents

Notes on Contributors

Marybexy Calcerrada Gutiérrez received her doctorate in the Philosophical Sciences from the Universidad Central de las Villas, Cuba. She is a Professor and Chair of the Department of Psychology at the Universidad de Holguín. She has published in both journals and edited volumes on gender identity, violence, and family from the perspective of philosophical anthropology articulated with a feminist worldview. She researches the democratization of human relations in emerging topics of micro-policy such as childhood, youth, and gender relations.

Miguel E. Bringuez Chacón graduated from the University of Holguín with his degree in Psychology in 2017. He now works in the private sector of the economy in Holguín, Cuba.

Alexander A. Cordovés Santiesteban earned his doctorate in Social Anthropology from the Universidade Federal de Santa Catarina in Florianopolis, Brazil. He is currently a Postgraduate Professor of Education at the Universidad Internacional Iberoamericana in Campeche, México (UNINI-Mx). He is a Collaborating Professor in the Postgraduate Program in Education at the Universidad Europea del Atlántico in Santander, Spain (UNEATLANTICO). His most recent research deals with trajectories of secondary school teachers in Cuban contexts and continuing education and training of teachers in Latin America. He also investigates topics in learning skills, strategic learning, and temporal organization with young adult university students in Cuba.

Sandra Fagales Mir is a Lecturer in the Department of Institutional Communication at the Universidad de Holguín, where she earned her B.A. in Journalism and a Master's in Culture and Identity Studies.

Carlos Manuel Osorio García is an Assistant Professor of Psychology at the Universidad de Holguín, Cuba. He earned his B.A. in Psychology from the Universidad de Holguín and his Master's in Social Work from the Universidad de Camagüey and completed his doctorate in Psychology at the University of Havana in 2021. He is also a member of the National Executive Board of the Cuban Society of Psychology and co-coordinator of the Provincial Network of Youth Research in Holguín. He holds the position of Chair of Educational Psychology and teaches Educational Psychology I and Special Needs Psychology. His principal lines of research include human learning and development in educational contexts and learning environments, temporal organization, and bullying.

Richard N. Gioioso is an Associate Professor of Political Science at Saint Joseph's University in Philadelphia, USA. In his research and writing, he examines the lives of Cuban young adults as they navigate economic, political, and social change on the island, in both the capital city, Havana, and the province of Holguín in eastern Cuba. He is also currently investigating political and legal philosophy in both historical and contemporary Cuba. He has written scholarly publications in *Urban Geography*, *The Latin Americanist*, *International Journal of Cuban Studies*, and *Latin American Law Review*. At Saint Joseph's University, he teaches a variety of courses with a focus on international relations, migration, and Latin American politics. In 2019, he was named recipient of the Junior Faculty Teaching Award by the Consortium of Latin American Studies Programs.

Miguel Rojas Gómez holds a doctorate in Philosophical Sciences (Cuba) and a doctorate in Philosophy (Colombia) and served as a professor at the Universidad Central de Las Villas in Santa Clara, Cuba. Currently, he is a professor of the Faculty of Fine Arts at the Universidad Pedagógica Nacional in Bogotá, Colombia. He has published as author and/or co-author more than thirty books, referring to Philosophy in Cuba and Latin America, Aesthetics and Art, Cultural Identity, and Integration.

Gloria Fariñas León received her Ph.D. in Psychological Sciences from the University of Lomonosov (Moscow) and her Ph.D. in Sciences from the Universidad de La Habana, from which she is a retired Professor and Vice President of the L. S. Vygotski Chair of the School of Psychology.

She is currently a Research Professor at the Universidad de La Salle (Bajío) and a member of the National Network of Researchers in Mexico. She is the author of seven books and several chapters in edited volumes and journal articles on issues in education, learning, and human development, as well as theoretical and methodological issues in the social sciences, especially psychology and education.

Zaily Leticia Velázquez Martínez is an Assistant Professor of Psychology at the Universidad de Holguín, Cuba, where she is currently the Chair of Organizational Psychology and the Head Professor of Development Psychology. She earned a B.A. in Psychology from the Universidad de Oriente and a Master's in Management from the Universidad de Holguín, where she will also finish her doctorate in Organizational Management. Her principal lines of research focus on personal interactions in organizations and the study of Cuban youth. She is also the co-coordinator of the Provincial Youth Network for Social Equity and a member of the executive committee of the provincial chapter of the Cuban Society of Psychology in Holguín.

Deysi E. García Rodríguez earned her Ph.D. in Psychology from the Universidade Federal de Santa Catarina in Florianopolis, Brazil. She is currently a Postgraduate Professor of Psychology at the Universidad Internacional Iberoamericana in Campeche, México (UNINI-Mx). She is a Collaborating Professor in the Postgraduate Program in Psychology at the Universidad Europea del Atlántico in Santander, Spain (UNEATLANTICO). Her current research focuses on topics in social psychology and the psychology of art: the subjectivization of time and the body. She also works on issues of lifestyle, temporal organization, learning, and subjectivity with young people in Cuban university environments.

Lisbet Almaguer Sao earned her B.A. in Psychology from the Universidad de Oriente (Santiago de Cuba) and her Master's in Social Sciences and Axiology from the Universidad de Holguín. She is currently an adjunct professor in the Department of Psychology at the Universidad de Holguín.

Aida T. Torralbas Fernández earned her B.A. in Psychology from the Universidad Central de Las Villas (Santa Clara, Cuba) and two Master's degrees, one in Clinical Psychology and the other in Gender Studies, from the Universidad de La Habana. She is an Assistant Professor of Psychology and member of the Gender Studies Working Group at the Universidad de Holguín.

Ania Pupo Vega is completing her doctoral studies in the postgraduate program in Political Sociology at the Universidade Federal de Santa Catarina (UFSC) in Florianopolis, Brazil. She earned her B.A. in Psychology from the Universidad Central de Las Villas and a Master's in Health Psychology from the Escuela Nacional de Salud in Havana, Cuba. Her research and publications focus on rural poverty from a gender perspective and public involvement in public management.

CHAPTER 1

Studying Youth and Development in Cuba

Richard N. Gioioso, Zaily Leticia Velázquez Martínez, and Carlos Manuel Osorio García

Introduction

Little has been written about how youth practices intersect with and are influenced by development—economic, human and social—and how youth as social actors negotiate and navigate development trends in Cuba. The collection of chapters we present in this book addresses issues relevant to young people, their experiences and participation in a variety of contexts. As young people constitute the future economic and social development of Cuba, analyzing the diversity of life experiences they face is a constant need for researchers, demanding attention to emerging

R. N. Gioioso (✉)
Saint Joseph's University, Philadelphia, PA, USA
e-mail: rgioioso@sju.edu

Z. L. V. Martínez · C. M. O. García
Universidad de Holguín, Holguín, Cuba
e-mail: zaily@uho.edu.cu

C. M. O. García
e-mail: cmosorio@uho.edu.cu

R. N. Gioioso et al. (eds.), *Youth and Development in Cuba*, https://doi.org/10.1007/978-3-030-90866-9_1

updates and contemporary contextualization. *Youth and Development in Cuba* advances social scientific knowledge and understanding with respect to various current *próblematiques* in the lives of young people who live on the island.

This book is a compilation of different theoretical approaches and current scientific research projects as we enter the 2020s. We address problems, situations, conflicts and development experiences over the last ten years related to young people from a part of Cuba far removed from the capital, in the third most populous city in the country, with a high impact cultural, tourist, educational, economic and social value for the entire island: the province of Holguín. Holguín's economic development is especially concentrated on tourism and nickel extraction, along with some industrial production. In recent decades, self-employment has appeared and expanded, opening up new forms of work for the entire population, but largely for young people. In addition, Holguín has a wide cultural movement recognized in national and foreign contexts for its activities in music, dance, theater and the plastic arts throughout the year.

The chapters that follow are the analyses of researchers whose specialize on Holguín with a specific locally situated focus, outside the most hegemonic discourses that emanate from Havana, the capital, where the largest number of publications are developed and as such portray Havana-centric visions that are generalized as truths and realities for the rest of the country. This book serves as useful reference material for scholars on youth, education and development in Cuba as well as for practitioners with youth in other related institutions and organizations. Thanks to strong international collaborations, we are able to present a wealth of social scientific studies from and about Holguín that serve to locate audiences within the Cuban framework of Holguín and to compare and contrast with the dynamics and realities of young people in other developing countries. Therefore, this collection serves to inform a wide audience in all regions of the Americas and outside the hemisphere.

One of the main contributions we make with this edited volume is the updated information about young people from eastern Cuba from different psychosocial perspectives. The information and analyses in this book allow comparisons to be made with the different situations and experiences of young people in other geographical areas of the country and in the Caribbean and Latin American regions. It also serves as a reference bibliography for students from different university majors and analysis for the development of scientific articles and undergraduate and postgraduate theses that address the nexus of young people and development in Cuba and other countries. In addition, it constitutes a preliminary diagnosis for the identification of possible problems to be solved by parents, relatives, educators and institutions in Holguín and in general, both inside and outside Cuba.

Our point of departure for *Youth and Development in Cuba* is a pluralistic understanding of youth(s)—that is, *juventud(es)* in Spanish—seen as an active generational subject, influenced socio-historically, as a kind of collective identity. By taking youth(s) into account, we demonstrate the diversity of social, economic, biological, personological, historical and psychological factors that intervene in the current *problématiques* of young people in Cuba's eastern province of Holguín. We also open roads to new directions to study and understand realities of and for youth there and elsewhere. We show the existence of regularities in the understanding of Cuban youth, and at the same time the need for contextualized interpretations framed in singular developmental spaces. It is a rupture of pre-established schemes and dogmas that highlights the need for multiple and complex visions of the same phenomenon from different positions and contexts.

The multiple views on contemporary issues presented in this volume are based on different and heterogeneous interpretations of the daily lives and experiences of young people. Our authors apply different approaches—such as gender theory, culture theory, psychology, education studies and sociology—to issues facing young people in Holguín. We have compiled this collection because we ourselves, as university professors, identified the need for updated literature that addresses the current problems of youth from a particular sociodemographic context. It enables debates on the epistemologies and methodologies used in youth studies. It offers the opportunity for scholars and practitioners from other countries a realistic vision of young people in a less-studied region of Cuba—Holguín—without the schematizations or distortions that can result from *a priori* conceptions. As such, it is a notable contribution to the existent bibliography in the field.

The Concept and Reality of the Study of Youth(s)

Researchers from multiple disciplines have delved into the characteristics of youth, their definition, typology, criteria for inclusion and other aspects that constitute debate in the study of youth(s). The definition of the concept has been peppered by multiple views, revealing the trend to prioritize age limits as a conditioning factor, although many analysts insist that there are more and broader criteria for the construction of *youth(s)* as a concept.

Among the most important experts in Cuba who have shaped the debate is the sociologist María Isabel Domínguez (1997, p. 68) whose point of departure is:

> a conception of youth defined as a historical-concrete category that designates an internally differentiated sociodemographic group according to its belonging to the social structure of society, in particular to the different classes and layers that compose it, while they constitute its most dynamic and mobile segment. We emphasize that youth is not biologically determined, but socially defined by the nature of the activity that takes place at that stage, which conditions a set of specific social relationships that shape youth status based on the meaning of that period. This constitutes a youth identity, which is both self-identity and identity recognized by members of other generations.

For her part, Cuban psychologist Laura Domínguez (2003) argues that youth has traditionally been defined as a transit age between childhood and adulthood. However, she criticizes the issue of age as a condition of youth and takes up some social issues that are decisive in this analysis, coinciding with the ideas previously discussed. In the following passage, she also highlights the importance of individual characteristics:

> [I]nstead of the universal schema, according to which belonging to a certain age determines once and for all the properties of young individuals, we must constantly take into account not only their chronological age, but also: 1) the general properties of the culture and society to which they belong; 2) their socio-economic position; 3) the historical situation in which its development occurs and the particularities of its generation (cohort); 4) their sex; and 5) their individual typological properties (p. 27).

At the international level, we find other perspectives on the subject, for example, Valenzuela (as cited in Alpízar & Bernal, 2003), who conceptualizes youth as "historically defined sociocultural construction" (p. 117) and Souto (2007) on the subject of its location by age range:

> Chronologically, it does not have precise age limits since, with the passage of time, there has been a process of expansion of these limits—which do not depend only on psychological considerations, but on social development, on the possibilities of economic and political independence, on legislation, or the perception of society and of young people themselves and youth organizations. (p. 171)

These researchers do not recognize the psychological as a determining factor of youth, an aspect that Domínguez (2003) does not tacitly affirm either, but rather they understand the social, cultural, historical and even the political (the normative, legislated) as elements of greater relevance in their understanding.

Souto's (2007), however, approaches youth as:

> … a social phenomenon [that] depends, rather than on age, on the position of the person in different social structures, among which the family, school, work and age groups stand out, and on the action of state institutions that with their legislation alter the position of young people in them. The existence of youth as a defined group is not a universal phenomenon and, like all age groups, its development, form, content and duration are social constructions and, therefore, historical, because they depend on the economic, social, cultural and political order of each society; that is, its historical location and the way in which "youth" is constructed in a society. (pp. 181–182)

Similarly, Taguenca (2009) recognizes the complexity in the theoretical and conceptual development of this construct of youth and the responsibility of society (the social) in its making, and tries to demonstrate that it will be in constant evolution and (re)elaboration. He echoes Levi and Schmitt (as cited in Taguenca, 2009: 161), viewing youth as:

> …something that never achieves a concrete and stable definition. Because therein resides both the burden of symbolic meanings, of promises and threats, of potentialities and fragilities that youth entails, as well as the ambiguous attention, constructed at the same time of hopes and suspicions, that in turn societies dedicate to it.

For his part, Brito (as cited in Taguenca, 2009: 166) coinciding with Domínguez's (1997) position regarding the low value of the biological, not the social, expresses that: "Youth is a social product, which we must differentiate from its biological conditioner." In both cases, the omission of the psychological aspect in the conception of youth is evident.

Carles Feixa (as quoted in Taguenca, 2009: 174) contributes further:

> For youth to exist, there must be, on the one hand, a series of social conditions such as norms, behaviors and institutions that distinguish youth from other age groups, and on the other hand, a series of cultural images: values, attributes and rites specifically associated with youth. Both of them depend on the social structure as a whole, that is, on the forms of subsistence, political institutions and ideological worldviews that predominate in each type of society.

This brief overview of some definitions of youth allows us to synthesize the following four ideas:

1. Age has traditionally been conceived as a criterion for inclusion of in the category of youth.
2. However, not only should biological and chronological criteria be considered, but also social criteria, e.g., the cultural, political, economic, historical, etc. In different contexts, these factors will have a significant impact on what will really define the youth.
3. As such, the understanding of youth demands the inclusion of diverse, pluralistic and heterogeneous approaches.
4. The psychological, i.e., what is subjectified by each individual, should be considered, as it permits fuller and more accurate understandings of young people as human beings.

We find an important need to follow such a path in the work of Alpízar and Bernal (2003), who argue that the theoretical perspectives employed in addressing youth have been carried out from homogenizing and stigmatizing positions, thus invisibilizing young women, devaluing the feminine, denying or not explaining the subjectivity of the researcher and a reliance on adult-centrism. It is therefore a challenge for current research to overcome these biased trends in youth analysis.

Regarding adult-centrism, Taguenca (2009) emphasizes that the adult is always marking what it is to be young, limiting the self-construction of youth, of being self-constructed youth, and conceives:

> The interrelations of youth with their significant others and with adults give rise to two types of youth: a differentiated one, unified generationally and communally, closed, in a struggle with the dominant culture, not liberating but transforming reality, at least in part; and the other imitative, assimilating the dominant culture, not transformative, but harmoniously integrated with the reproductive social processes. (p. 181)

From our point of view, this classification skews somewhat the diverse, pluralistic and heterogeneous understanding of youth we are trying to promote. Specifically, we disagree with Taguenca's idea of only two types of youth, limited to their capacities to transform or not the social processes that engulf them. From our perspective, these processes should not be seen in black and white, but rather with a recognition of their nuances. We identify more with the vision of Villa (2011), who supports the use of multiple criteria in defining youth, which allows youth to be understood as a process that becomes human-social. Thus, there are various ways of being young that prescribe that, in the analysis of the human-social, it is necessary to refer to youth (pp. 150–151).

To close this section, we echo Duarte's (2000) proposal of four valuable clues for understanding youth:

1. Youth refers to the need to learn to see youth as bearers of differences and singularities that build their plurality and diversity in different social spaces.
2. Employing and producing kaleidoscopic understandings toward and from youth allows us to capture the wealth of the aforementioned plurality.
3. Direct and intimate connection with youth in their diverse and pluralistic worlds is a necessary condition for the creation of comprehensive knowledge.
4. The goal in the study of youth is not to construct totalizing and universalizing categories, but rather dynamic and flexible concepts that progressively approach the subjects of study: young people, expressions of youthfulness, and the processes of becoming and being youths.

In the following section, we explore the fundamental approach employed by many of the authors in this compilation, rooted in Psychology: the Cultural-Historical approach. It is important for us to explore because it emerged from the Marxist approach, which undergirds the contemporary Cuban academy.

The Cultural-Historical Approach to the Study of Youth(s) in and from Cuba

Regardless of the studies carried out in Cuba and the existence of the Code of Childhood and Youth in the country,[1] debate and theoretical-methodological production that deepens the complexity of youth must continue and be developed. Thus, we provide a treatment of the subject using the Historical-Cultural approach, a theoretical-methodological perspective that predominates in research carried out mainly in Cuba and Latin America, originating in the ideas of Liev Semionovich Vygotski (1896–1934), its founder and first theorist. In order to understand, explain and transform the human being, Vygotski began to build and elaborate a psychological theory and practice[2] based on the dialectical and historical materialism developed by Karl Marx (Corral, 2006).

Soviet Psychology and the Cultural-Historical approach began in force among Cuban researchers in the 1970s when a group of them went to carry out their doctoral studies in the Soviet Union.[3] The creation of the L. S. Vygotski Honorary Chair of the Faculty of Psychology of the University of Havana in October 1998 consolidated the presence of the approach in Cuba.[4]

For Vygotski and the Cultural-Historical approach, all human behavior is social in nature, since the psychological originates from social interactions (Ratner, 2013). This is explained from a system of principles, laws and categories that include: the social situation of development, the experience, the genetic law of development, personality and the activity-communication system, among others.

In his book on the History of Psychology, Corral (2006) summarizes the foundations of the approach in four axioms:

1. On the evolutionary scale, man separates himself from animals as he transforms his reality. As this happens, the subject transforms himself, developing from a process of education-self-education, and as such the active character of human beings and their dual effect on society and on himself is highlighted.
2. Activity is mediated by instruments. The production and registration of instruments is what differentiates man from other living beings. In this axiom, it is especially relevant to recognize the mediated

nature of human behavior, since what is generated is an instrument-mediated relationship between human beings and their actions, as well as between the person and the environment.

3. Man's activity is only transformative and mediated in conditions of social relations. Social and personal transformation is achieved in cooperation, so it is necessary to deploy an activity-communication system that reproduces and produces cultural and social heritage. Social relationships are established with others who serve as zones of potential development in the transformation process, that is, as more capable others, who can motivate personal development. At this point the Genetic Law of Development is presented as a process of enculturation and subjectivation that consists of:

   > …any function in the child's cultural development appears on the scene two times, on two levels: first as something social, then as something psychological; first among people as an interpsychic category, then within the child as an intrapsychic category (Vygotski, 1987, p. 161).

   Thus, all content that the subject appropriates, subjectivizes and learns is a social domain that is transformed into capacity and self-control of personal behavior that expresses the development of the subject. This process of enculturation and subjectivation declares the active role of subjects in their own development and in social, economic and cultural development in general.[5]

4. The last axiom is that the domain of human behavior is the history of the domain of behavior. Historicity as an explanatory principle is essential in psychological analysis and in the analysis of human development. For Corral (2006), there are at least four stories to unravel in the emergence of the human being: the phylogenetic history of the human species; the social and collective history of human society; the ontogenetic history of the individual; and micro-history, that is, the history of a specific process in personal evolution. All of these stories converge and intertwine in human beings, a situation that presents itself as *personality*, as a unique and unrepeatable subject active in the construction of his history and personal development.

The theoretical-methodological value of the categories, laws and principles have made this approach transcendent in Cuba and Latin America. One of the contributions of the approach, which has made this transcendence possible, is the understanding of the interrelationship between education and human development, an idea that Fariñas (2005: 8) highlights as follows: "For culturalist historians, the explanation of human behavior as expression of personality and also its improvement must be found in the education-development relationship." This relationship is relevant in studies with subjects at different stages of development and particularly with young people when they begin their university or trade studies, among others that imply greater independence.

In his investigations, Vygotski (2003) observed a diversity in the theories of learning that led him to introduce the zone of proximal development principle, through which he explains how personal development emerges from processes of education-self-education, that is, how education leads, pushes and pull development. He argues: "Our hypothesis establishes the unity, not the identity, of the learning processes and the processes of internal development. This supposes that the one becomes the other" (59).

To briefly explain the interrelationship between learning and development, we expound on what Vygotski (1987: 151) understands by development in his approach:

> A complex dialectical process, characterized by a multiple periodicity, by a disproportion in the development of the different functions, by metamorphoses or qualitative transformations of some forms into others, by the complicated interweaving of the processes of evolution and of involution, by the intertwined relationship between internal and external factors and by the intricate process of overcoming difficulties.

This position is far from biology-centric, pondering the complexity of development instead of an aspect of it. As can be seen, development does not have a linear character, but rather is characterized by processes of evolution and involution where internal and external contradictions play a central role. That is, development does not depend exclusively on biological, psychological or social processes, but these processes must converge dialectically in conditions of education.

Research from the Cultural-Historical approach considers the education-development relationship based upon what Vygotski called the social situation of the development of the subject or members of the group, community, society, company, etc. As explained by Fariñas (2005), this is, as a macro category in the approach, a:

> …special combination of the internal processes of development and external conditions, which is typical at each stage and which also conditions the dynamics of psychic development during the corresponding evolutionary period and the new, qualitatively peculiar psychological formations that emerge towards the end of said period.[6]

The unfailing relationship between internal processes and external conditions faced by the subject highlights the infinite possibilities and diversity that can lead to development. For Fariñas (2005: 57), the social situation of development "is the active relationship of the individual with his environment, in other words, a subjective elaboration in which the environment is only one of his starting points."

The arrival at a new social development situation in which subsequent human development occurs and is sustained is what Fariñas (2005) calls development. This is explained in the Cultural-Historical approach from the beginning zone of proximal development, conceived as:

> …the distance between the actual level of development, determined by the ability to independently solve a problem, and the potential level of development, determined through the resolution of a problem under the guidance of an adult or in collaboration with another more capable partner (Vygotski, 2003: 53–54).

The system of laws, categories and principles developed by Vygotski's Cultural-Historical approach highlights its theoretical-methodological utility for the study of youth in the social sciences because it explains the unique and unrepeatable character in the personal development of each young person utilizing the processes of institutional education (or not) as well as self-education. In turn, it recognizes the dialectical and historical character of this development, as well as the consideration of internal processes and external conditions as axes in this human development.

Thus, *Youth and Development in Cuba* both highlights the importance and relevance of the Cultural-Historical approach for studies on youth(s) and in employing it is distinct from other scholarly publications about Cuban young people by Cuban and foreign researchers alike. The kaleidoscopic lenses used in this compilation have been developed in Cuba for more than 50 years, based on Marxist principles that have shaped the Cuban political, economic, social and cultural environment. In short, the perspectives presented here represent a kind of decolonization of knowledge about Cuban youth(s) and are useful for informing new perspectives to the study of youth environments and their practices.

Structure of the Book

This edited volume has been conceived of and designed to offer the reader a combination of chapters written by experts in youth studies in Cuba, with a special focus on youth in the province of Holguín in eastern Cuba. The contributions are conceptual, theoretical-methodological and empirical. The authors are part of a group made up of academics who are at various stages of their professional lives, from those who are currently completing their doctoral studies to the status of professor emerita. Thus, this collection allows a view of the creation of the newest and most innovative ideas and perspectives of those who are beginning their careers together with contributors who have been involved in the study of youth(s) in Cuba for more than three decades. Many authors live in Holguín and work at the University of Holguín, while others are outside the country, in Mexico, Brazil and the United States.

A compilation like this one, which facilitates the emergence of the contributions of experts from Holguín on Holguín, accessible as a whole and to the English-speaking and international world, is rare. As the third most populous city in Cuba and a center of people, industry, art and tourism, Holguín serves as a locus of study of the dynamics and processes of change and transformation that young people live, face and promote in the urban context. It is also useful for examining these issues in a rural context. The chapters that follow deal with a variety of current and important topics for young Cuban-*holguineros* themselves and for the society of the province and of Cuba generally.

In Chapter 2, Gloria Fariñas, an expert in Educational Psychology and youth education, offers an analysis of the challenges young people face in contemporary sociocultural development. She identifies and addresses the most fundamental ones, which include the volume of knowledge to be built, the ability to think complexly and dialectically about such construction, and the importance of cultivating criticality and operating creatively in order to achieve a better world for all. In the second part of the chapter, she analyzes some solutions to these demands in the fields of education and social participation. Next, she presents the results of a research project aimed at promoting the autonomy of young people as a fundamental indicator of human development. Finally, she analyzes the particularities of the demands for Cuban youth and solutions to the project of cultural and socioeconomic development in Cuba in a context of globalization.

From the Department of Psychology of the University of Holguín, Marybexy Calcerrada and Miguel Rojas Gómez offer a critical reflection on the analysis of expressions of cultural violence in youth. In Chapter 3, they analyze social conditions with cultural significance—urban and rural, race and gender—with respect to power relations, the expression of authentic culture or culture of domination, and the identification of racism, sexism, ethnocentrism, and hegemonic and subordinate identities as manifestations of violence. As such, they offer cultural criteria for the recognition of violence in youth and synthesize expressions of symbolic violence among a sample of this population in Holguín.

In Chapter 4, entitled *Espacios que pesan*/Spaces that Matter: (Re)thinking Youth in Rural Holguín, Ania Pupo examines the relationships between the category of *space*—focusing on rural areas—and its relevance to youth studies in general, and specifically in the examination of youth in Holguín. Based on research results carried out in communities in Holguín, she emphasizes the essentiality of the analytical force of the *space* category for the understanding of contextual elements that determine the departure of young people from Holguín as they (de)configure themselves in aging and masculinized spaces. She highlights these elements as crucial factors in local economic dynamics and explains the challenges to the implementation of policies capable of transforming the contexts—based on the perceptions, representations and narratives of their populations gathered through fieldwork—into spaces of life and work.

In Chapter 5, Deysi E. García and Alexander A. Cordovés, who specialize in aspects of learning in Cuban university contexts, offer us critical reflections on methodological dialogues for the practice of science with life. They propose a systematization of research *on/with* young people, identifying achievements, possibilities and inadequacies as possible frameworks for other research. They combine Butler's (2015) perspective of framing, Bakhtin's (2012 [1924]) participant thinking as an act of empathy and Zanella's (2017) proposals to move from studies *about* youth to studies *with* youth to argue in favor of an ethical and dialogical position in the production of knowledge. They analyze their own practices of teaching and researching about Cuban young people to propose possible framings *with* young people. Thus, two lines of work stand out: teaching and research that assumes a historical understanding of development and that which creates conditions for studying development. Both find foundations in the Cultural-Historical approach proposed by Vygotski.

In Chapter 6, we, the editors, present the results of an empirical study that reveal the intersections between temporal organization and life projects in a group of Cuban youth. Using a dialectical research-analysis-writing approach, professors Zaily Velázquez and Carlos Osorio of the University of Holguín collaborate with their former student, Miguel E. Bringuez, and colleague Richard Gioioso in the United States to examine the ability to create and execute the temporal organization of daily activities in the necessary way that leads to the successful achievement of life projects in a group of young art instructors in the province of Holguín. Results show that participants spend most of their time in the family and work spheres, which constitute the main contents of their life projects, together with emigration as an aspiration and response to current economic deficiencies, and the need for fellowship and intimacy with close relatives. However, data suggest there is a lack of critical and generalized temporary organization that would make it possible to carry out these projects to fruition.

From their points of view as professors and researchers at the University of Holguín, Aida T. Torralbas and Sandra Fagales present in Chapter 7 the results of their study with Journalism students at the University of Holguín about their conceptions of gender violence against women in couple's relationships. In Cuba, the symbolic subordination that exists of one gender over another is not usually recognized, causing invisibility of the imbalance of power between the sexes. This is the fundamental basis of violent relationships, and ignorance of these dynamics facilitates their reproduction in both the personal and professional spheres. The results of the research Torralbas and Fagales present suggest that there is a misunderstanding about and an ignorance of gender violence as well as the power relations that underlie it.

The collection closes with a chapter by Lisbet Almaguer Sao, inspired by her experiences in her practice of clinical psychology. In a study on subjective well-being and human development by the Department of Psychology of the University of Holguín, 55 young adult participants exhibited the presence of an existential crisis. These included the identification of intra- and inter-personal conflicts, frustrations, contradictions and crises in some areas of personality, and they serve as the platform for Almaguer Sao to consider existential crises in the lives of young people in Holguín using the Cultural-Historical approach.

Thus, we leave a varied collection of chapters on youth(s) in Cuba that cover the conceptual, theoretical-methodological and the empirical. Geographically, they focus on the province of Holguín, in eastern Cuba, since the core of the team of contributors to this volume lives there and works at the University of Holguín. Together they have been able to establish a study site for young people in the area regarding various dimensions of their psychological, social and economic development. The great contribution of the book is to define a space on youth(s) in Cuba outside the capital, analyzed mainly by experts from the area, that reaches the international public in the English language.

Notes

1. In Article 1, the Code of Childhood and Youth (*Código de la Niñez y la Juventud*) in Cuba regulates the participation of children and young people under thirty years of age in the construction of the new society and establishes the obligations of the people, organizations and institutions that intervene in their education, in accordance with the objective of promoting the formation of the communist personality in the young generation. Article 2 states that this code is part of the socialist legal order; therefore, the exercise of rights and compliance with the obligations established by current legislation, in relation to children and youth, must comply with the provisions of its regulations.
2. This approach has been very useful in the educational sciences, anthropology, among others. See Lave and Wenger (1991) for an example.
3. Nevertheless, they were used beginning in 1967 in the Enrique José Varona Pedagogical Institute of Havana, in psychology texts by Smirnov and Leontiev used in Cuba (personal communication, María Febles, May 9, 2020).
4. The creation of the Chair materialized due to the proposal made by those attending the I and II Conferences on the legacy of the Cultural-Historical approach that were held in 1996 and 1998

respectively (personal communication, Guillermo Arias, May 5, 2020).
5. See Zinchenko (1990: 200).
6. As cited in Bozhovich (1976: 123).

Bibliography

Alpízar, L., & Bernal, M. (2003). La construcción social de las juventudes. *Última Década, 19*, 105–123.

Bakhtin, M. (2012 [1924]). *Para uma filosofia do ato responsável* (2nd ed., V. Viotello & C. A. Faraco, Trans.). Pedro & João Editores.

Bozhovich, L. I. (1976). Psychological regularities of personality formation in childhood. *Issues in Psychology, 6*, 45–53.

Butler, J. (2015). *Quadros de guerra: quando a vida é passível de luto?* Civilização Brasileira.

Corral, R. (2006). *Historia de la Psicología: Apuntes para su estudio*. Editorial Universitaria Félix Varela.

Domínguez, L. (2003). *Psicología del Desarrollo: Adolescencia y juventud*. Editorial Universitaria Félix Varela.

Domínguez, M. I. (1997). La juventud en el contexto de la estructura social cubana. Datos y reflexiones. *Temas, 52*, 67–81.

Duarte, K. (2000). ¿Juventud o juventudes? Acerca de cómo mirar y remirar a las juventudes de nuestro continente. *Última Década, 13*, 59–77.

Fariñas, G. (2005). *Psicología, educación y sociedad. Un estudio sobre el desarrollo humano*. Félix Varela.

Lave, J., & Wenger, E. (1991). *Situated learning: Legitimate peripheral participation*. Cambridge University Press.

Ratner, C. (2013). *Desde Vygotski a la Psicología Macrocultural*. Documenta Universitaria.

Souto, S. (2007). Juventud, teoría e historia: La formación de un sujeto social y de un objeto de análisis. *Historia Actual Online, 13*, 171–192.

Taguenca, J. A. (2009). El concepto de juventud. *Revista Mexicana De Sociología, 71*(1), 159–190.

Villa, M. E. (2011). Del concepto de juventud al de juventudes y al de lo juvenil. *Revista De Educación y Pedagogía, 23*(60), 147–157.

Vygotski, L. (1987). *Historia del desarrollo de las funciones psíquicas superiores*. Editorial Científico Técnica.

Vygotski, L. (2003). Interacción entre aprendizaje y desarrollo. In G. A. Martínez Campos & M. E. Rodríguez Pérez (Eds.), *Psicología del desarrollo escolar. Selección de lecturas* (Vol. 1, pp. 45–59). Editorial Universitaria Félix Varela.

Zanella, A. (2017). *Entre galerias e museus: diálogos metodológicos no encontro da arte com a ciência e a vida*. Pedro & João Editores.

Zinchenko, P. (1990). Entrevista al Dr. en Psicología Vladímir Petróvich Zínchenko. En M. Shuare. *La psicología soviética tal como yo la veo*. Editorial Progreso.

CHAPTER 2

On the Challenges Facing Young People in Contemporary Sociocultural Development

Gloria Fariñas León

Contemporary Society and Its Demands on Young People

When thinking about the future of society, one should always think especially about young people. Youth is a key age in which important social and personal commitments are taken on, but in order to do that, young people must be comfortable with themselves. They must know how to meet the demands of society and in so doing satisfy their personal material and spiritual needs, including those of prosperity and living well. Youth and society must find paths of convergence in which public policies on education and employment play a critical role. Moreover, analyzing this situation requires examining the subject–world or subject–society relationships through the lens of the common good (Hinkelammert,

This chapter was translated by Doralkis Ramírez Ronda.

G. F. León (✉)
Universidad de La Habana, Havana, Cuba

R. N. Gioioso et al. (eds.), *Youth and Development in Cuba*,
https://doi.org/10.1007/978-3-030-90866-9_2

2006). Therefore, the ethical choice is the compass that indicates the way to living well, not the relativist prediction of "anything goes" of postmodernism.

There are many demands on youth and meeting them involves addressing issues from both the young person's point of view and that of the educator (Manacorda, 1987). The *educator* is often thought of as an agent of change to the content of teaching and the ways that she or he performs the educational action. In this scenario, the actor cannot be separated from the work he or she does or from its content. An educator who promotes a "reproductive education" cannot truly be an agent of change. These challenges in educator–student relations demand an authentic and democratic relationship between them, which is easy to say, but much more difficult to fully achieve given present living conditions. However, it is necessary to clarify them in order to pursue them consciously. Thus, in the section that follows, I will consider two major issues for analysis.

> *First: What demands must young people meet in order to properly insert themselves in the development of society so that they can bring about their own personal development?*

An educator must act in sync with the demands I mention above. Accordingly, I will refer to my colleagues' and my own experience as a professor and researcher of Cuban college students, as well as my experience with Mexican college students with whom I am currently working. Although I will make some observations relevant to young people generally, the focus on my analysis is contemporary Cuban reality.[1]

Every society has either explicit or implicit aspirations about the model of human being that it wishes to develop, and the contours of the model manifest themselves differently in each historical period, even though members of society are not fully aware of it at the time. Societies have a cultural identity that does not rule out their diversity; there are essential, enduring characteristics that are updated with the new demands of life and human knowledge, e.g., the mind-boggling technological changes caused by the advent of the internet and social media. We can talk about Latin American-ness or Cuban-ness even though the current meaning of the concepts is not identical to that of 100 years ago. There is a history, however, that even with its vicissitudes, identifies human beings in cultural spaces and times. These demands exist for all young people; however, only those who can fulfill them will be able to meet both social and personal needs convergently.

In his essay *Nuestra América* (Our America), José Martí (1962) argued that universities should educate human beings so that they can fly beyond their time, i.e., to know how to bring about the future and transcend, allowing the metaphor of the winged man who identifies the future to emerge (Navarro, 2006). But this idea of the human being is not unexpected in Martí, who was born in 1853, the same year that Félix Varela[2] (1853)—the man who taught Cubans how to think—died. Martí was a perpetuator of the ideas of Varela and other Cuban patricians as well. The history of Cuba has a fertile repertoire of ideas on the model of human being for the nation, from the first heroes to the present day. In the analysis of historical sources such as those by Rodríguez (2005) and Torres (2002, 2006), the most outstanding minds of the eighteenth and nineteenth centuries can be identified, among them creole ideologues such as Francisco de Arango y Parreño (1765–1837) and José Agustín Caballero (1762–1835), who reflected on the psychosocial characteristics of the Cuban people and their duties. In addition, José Antonio Saco y López Cisneros (1797–1879)—the illustrious follower of Varela—who recognized the role of education in social development; likewise, making the Cuban identity known, he opposed the annexationist trend with the United States of America. José de la Luz y Caballero,[3] in particular, was renowned for his educational activity and as the "mind disruptor," and whom Martí especially admired (Torres, 2006). All of them were precursors to and served as the breeding ground for the ideas and actions of Carlos Manuel de Céspedes[4] in 1868 who worked to bring about Cuban independence from Spain.

In contemporary times, we remember the ideas of other prominent Cubans like Ernesto "Che" Guevara (1967)—Argentinian by birth—with his political-philosophical essay *Socialism and Man in Cuba*. Likewise, we recall the ideas of Fidel Castro (2007) in *History will absolve me* about the need for an educated man, one that is multilaterally and integrally developed, and the weighing of subjective conditions in the development of society (Castro, 2004). The ideas of Roberto Fernández (2000) in *Todo Calibán* emphasized the distinction of the non-colonized human being. In the works of these actors of Cuban history and culture, we find life paths that share an invariable essence: a cultured human being who works in a revolutionary way and committed to the common good.

Revolutionary, in this sense, refers to being transformative, without a colonized mentality, working for the common good in a society that is increasingly closer to equity, far from any egalitarianism that distorts the understanding and legitimization of human diversity.

This collection of ideas stands out because it is as valid for the present as it is for the future, not only in the southern hemisphere, but also in the global north. In reviewing Herbert Marcuse's (2016) essay *One-Dimensional Man*, we can perceive the image of that human being, either male or female, that restricts his or her own development. By following the absolute commands of merchandize, we expel critical concepts, perceiving culture—and therefore spirituality too—as a trivial consumer item or a temporary-use product without significant transcendence even for good taste, and with the main purpose of entertainment or hedonism, although these goes against the true aesthetic enjoyment that broadens and enriches our intelligence and sensibilities. For Mancuse (2016, p. 21), "… democracy consolidates domination more firmly than absolutism…," as it consolidates the control of the market over people. Reality is the reality of the businessman, a type of democracy that is not emancipating at all.

In order to understand the attainment of the liberating goals for human beings, we need to point out a set of supporting dimensions: that ideal is not automatically achieved, and not only based on fortuitous personal achievements or specific didactic methodologies applicable in a standardized manner to all groups of students. These dimensions of personal and social formation point to the struggle for the decolonization of imaginaries, especially those of young people and their educators, who are also young, or were young not so long ago. According to Roland Barthes (1973), the decolonization of thought and action is what makes us gain freedom. Therefore, it is not by accident that I have introduced this chapter with a reflection grounded in these thinkers' ideas. In theory, we require a culture (epistemological, ethical, aesthetic, political, among other dimensions) anchored in the universal values of the common good and that legitimizes the invisible in the current conditions of neocolonization on an astral scale.

The utopia of the human being, understood not in a pejorative sense but as an aspiration or compass that guides education, needs concrete fulfillment, which can be summarized in a set of requirements of human development at present, namely:

Complex Dialectical Thinking in Southern Epistemology

It means overcoming the fragmentary and simplifying or linear vision of reality phenomena and processes, in the field of professional knowledge or of everyday life, for the sake of a dialectical vision about the complexity of reality as a whole. The positive vision, turned into prevailing positivism, has led human scientific understanding or of common sense, to fully judge and classify what is only seen in a fragmented or partial way, thus limiting the view of its total historical character. This perspective borders on Manichaeism and prejudice, which does not allow us to value the different nuances of reality and human positions before it. It is necessary to understand the scientific and technological development as a wise condition for good living, the common good and the solidarity-based construction of the future; in other words, to give rise to knowledge practices that allow social transformation, not the status quo produced by merchandize and entrepreneurs. It takes a lot of educational formation to judge world or local events from more than a simple perception. It is necessary to look behind the multiple historical contradictions that hide behind appearances; it must go from the phenomenon to the essence.

This points to a change in paradigm, the bases of which were created by Karl Marx and other visionary intellectuals (Eagleton, 2018). Nevertheless, it is necessary to carry out new readings and analyses because the reality that he foresaw is presented to us today in very diverse modalities, although its essence persists. We must read diverse sources written by those who have dedicated themselves to study the current cultural phenomena and processes and their consequences, the absent or ignored realities, the realities of current colonization, which is primarily oriented toward the cultural aspect. This is the reason why a southern epistemology is necessary, although it is not geographically located below the Equator.

Criticality and Creativity: For Sustainable Development

Young people, in order to become the main force in the progress of any society and of themselves, ought to be good readers both of letters and of reality. This means that they need to be critical readers able to appropriately carry out the development project of the country in view of new realities, ideas and practices—or the conditions to produce them—aiming at attaining a better world for Cubans and for all of humanity regardless of creed and race, being aware of the need of preserving the environment, peace and dialogue, which are necessary before the irrefutable contrivances or fourth generation war.[5] Thus, it is unavoidable to know that in order to achieve it, the longing for knowledge that widens horizons without mental schemes, by reading different materials, even the antagonistic ones, is necessary. This liberates one's viewpoint and reflection of the type of Manichaeism that is typical of extremist individuals of any ideological orientation; dogmatism can be found in the actors of all schools of thought. The task is to know how to identify and overcome this. Likewise, to know how to properly question and support the ideas, given the fact that questioning could counteract, up to a certain extent, the possibility of snobbishness. Besides, it is critical to note that criticism conveys a decolonized point of view.

Criticism demands knowledge of professional discipline and of the disciplines that bestow this knowledge—or any other—with an integrated dimension in a world conception such as Philosophy and History. In this globalized world, it is virtually impossible to achieve a critical point of view and to overlook the origin and development of the present world situation or the specific relations among countries and among people.

Reality has become rather uncertain because it is very often intentionally distorted so as to give it a coat of make up or discredit it. Although information manipulation can happen in every political stance, there should be discernment between things that are essential things and those that are superfluous. Such discernment is allowed by basic historical and philosophical knowledge for the analytical and rational management of the different sources of information in terms of crossed reading. The diverse information that saturates the human perspective of reality (Gergen, 1992) at present, must be identified and critically reintegrated as well as dismantled by analyzing its roots. It is necessary for all social actors to observe certain precautions, not just young people. Southern epistemology arose (de Sousa Santos, 2012) to give a surname to the complexity approach born from dialectic logic, which has acquired some preponderance in Latin America. Such epistemology also has its ethical and historical character. *Our North is the South*, reads the advertising slogan of Telesur[6]; of course, one needs to look, or even better, to know how to look at another north, either from the West or from the East.

No science or discipline is aseptic; sociocultural and personal interests crisscross all of them. As such, one must take a position. I do not advocate discarding the information, its analysis or enjoyment; this would mean allowing ourselves to fall into the arms of the rampant dogmatism that is as improper as snobbishness. Barthes (1973), when dealing with the problematic of literature, especially novels, pointed out that the aim of a novel and that of a narrated story is to alienate the facts, which obeys the mythology of the universal, which is characteristic of the capitalist society that sustains it as a cultural product, through which it imposes its values to all. Of course, I do not advocate reading in a limited fashion, but to read with a sense of criticality. I advocate for youth to become readers who know how to dig and search behind the fact or the appearance with which one can be delighted, without naivety.

The pleiad of Cuban intellectuals who have contributed to the development of national critical thinking with theoretical essays is endless, although we can mention an anthology of contemporary authors summarized by Hernández (2015),[7] which includes figures such as Martínez, Sánchez, Arboleya, Rodríguez, War, Fornet, Fernandez, Alonso, Alzugaray, Barcia, de la Torre, Dominguez, among others. Their knowledge of the history of Cuba, America and the world is remarkable. This history is not really known if there is lack of knowledge of the history of the countries of America as a whole and their relations with the Old World throughout the history of the continent; and in the same way, the universal of colonialism and neocolonialism.

There is a resolution to defend both critical reading and the restless readers who know how to look for the significant literature in all possible sources, also pondering those who, as citizens, are part of their own history. In other words, for a young Cuban, the knowledge of Cuban thought is crucial to his or her development up to the present time along with the most important foreign schools of thought. It does not matter that the academy does not emphasize them. Good sources of reading should be sought out—what is being published about such topics—to know in which Cuban and foreign journals good and new ideas can be found. It also takes reading everything we can consider crosscurrent.

Having intellectual solvency (Pogolotti, 2015) is necessary to be well-informed and to be able to cross-reference the sources of information. This is not a time to agree with everything, and really, no time has been so; but arguments should be formulated and stated in a complete, complex and dialectical way. On the other hand, criticality and creativity make up a dynamic unity; there is no point in emptying one from the other. Shallow criticism has no prospective meaning; the fact that deep criticality leads to relevant changes favored by creativity is what makes it important. To determine where and when there is manipulation of information also implies a critical and creative approach to reality. That solvency embodies knowledge, criticality and creativity.

The Domain of Relevant Information in the Society of Knowledge

In the midst of chaotic information—namely technical, epistemological, scientific, artistic, among others—in correspondence with the demands of personal and social life, it is not possible to process it outside of a critical point of view. Therefore, it is mandatory to adopt a position to be able to discern between what is relevant and irrelevant, true and essential, and false or trivial. It is not just about being well informed, but also about analyzing the contradictions and the significance of the information for the permanent elaboration and re-elaboration of a point of view in order to enrich it. Likewise, it is not about a literal understanding of the word but of a critical reading that is proactive at the same time.

The diluted literature to which several editorials accustom readers separates them from relevant information and trivialize knowledge, leaving them unprepared to understand complex problems. The uncritical or uneducated reader may form an opinion from an immediate literal reading, when what is involved is to know how to separate the "chaff from the wheat." This intrinsically relates with the tendency to judge and classify in a totalizing way what is only partially seen or fragmented. In order to carry out a good critical reading, the reader must know how to distinguish the sources of information from their motivations and the ideological preference of the authors and publishers to identify the spectrum of the information.

To have knowledge is not limited to the mastery of technique in rapid development—this would be a simplification of knowledge—but to have a certain cultural heritage and intellectual capacity based on a critical and creative reading that includes technique. Bill Gates, from Microsoft, is not smarter than Archimedes or Da Vinci were in their times. If one aspires to a core reading of reality and of the printed or electronic letter, its synonym is educated reading.

Educational Alternatives for Comprehensive Solutions

As pointed out at the beginning of this chapter, the problem of young people cannot be addressed apart from education and employment opportunities. Any solution outside these two conditions alienates the perspective to incorporate and keep young people anchored in society and its culture, since study and work are the social mechanisms to achieve and maintain such inclusion. It is not about getting a job without skills, or about skills without employment; both aspects must be addressed as a unit. Although in Cuba the alternatives of training and qualifications have been diversified, this refers to the situation of university young people, and within this group to those who had not been able to gain access to university studies because they did not have a professional job or because they had an illicit one. It is not just a matter of incorporating them, but of the type of education that they should all receive in order to promote the targeted development to become agents of change. It is then necessary to ask the second question:

> *What requirements must education fulfill, especially university education, so that young people can be properly involved in the development of society, and satisfy their needs for both material and spiritual development?*

In order to answer this question, both the requirements and the current obstacles that can divert university education from its best courses must be analyzed; and the starting point in order to evaluate them should emanate from an historical perspective:

> First of all, we must recognize the political ideology about culture and social development of the ideologists of Cuban nationality since the eighteenth century, although with emphasis on the decisive nineteenth century for the history of Cuba—among which José Martí reached a more explicit and long-lasting Latin American dimension—extending to the present day. The development of education in Cuba today (Arias, 2005; Torres, 2006) finds its foundation in all this ideology, mainly from the nineteenth to the twentieth centuries. Secondly, in the foundation created by contemporary authors who, with their research and theoretical-methodological formulations,

> consolidated the conceptions that could lead to these aspirations in culture and education, granting them equal universality and scientific character. The main contributions can be found in the work of the founding historical and cultural Soviet psychologists and collaborators; and that of Guillermo Arias (2005), Ana María Siverio and Josefina López (1991), and mine—Gloria Fariñas (2006), among other authors, in Cuba.

Education aiming at developing critical, creative, therefore revolutionary human beings needs to be transformative, so that it brings about:

General and Comprehensive Training

Traditionally, Cuba has been open to the best of universal culture, to advances in scientific, technical, literary and artistic thought, even more so since generalizing education and employment opportunities after 1959, a date that marked a new milestone in the history of the country. Even in times of a precarious economy, the need to save culture has been satisfied in some way, and has top priority in public development policy. However, cultural development is not for entertainment or enjoyment alone (Freire, 2006), but rather to expand cultural exposure and learning for a sustainable social development.

The Cuban development project is oriented toward sustainability; and one of the most outstanding aspects of current improvement of university curriculum is its flexibility. This guarantees a general constant of national education in all universities, as well as its adjustment to the peculiarities of the region, locality and the development they require. Likewise, each plan of study carries the flexibility of systematic updating of contents, even annually if necessary.

Development of the Critical Reader

Critical reading, that is, non-colonized, demands a body of general background knowledge, especially a philosophical and historical knowledge, not only within the academic curriculum; and its academic attention should add sufficient incentive for students to autonomously seek out more sources of information and knowledge beyond the walls of the academy. Although the academy fosters access to information, other sociocultural media are in charge of expanding and supporting access. Cuban critique is entrenched in the internationalist vision, but not the annexation of internal and external relations. Such annexationist currents have been a great problem for the nation and served as a central obstacle to the sovereignty of Cuba. This is a point that Saco clarified until his last days, and which was later taken up again by ideologues and patriots (Torres, 2006). The condition of annexation has taken different forms since the nineteenth century, and still it remains in the twenty-first century, under the apparel of the fourth-generation war, observable through the media of the central powers on a daily basis.

Education must also be effective in using the necessary means for these purposes, but it should be intelligent at the same time, since one of the current camouflages of colonized and annexationist visions is the alleged dogmatism attributed to these precautions. Cuban critical thinkers have acknowledged that criticality is oriented above all to name and un-do colonization in all its forms, as friendly as they may appear. Criticism is historical and cultural; it is expressed from a certain position and, if it is professional, it must be consciously exercised from a conception that is both philosophical—taking into consideration of all its approaches and fields of knowledge for its understanding—and historical, meaning it is understood in a non-anecdotal manner, but rather in one with a particular emphasis on the history of the global south, which is more social and cultural than geographical.

The Complex Dialectical Vision of Reality

To a large extent, education fulfills the comprehensive formation of the young university student by fostering a construction of knowledge on the basis of a perspective of dialectical complexity—including southern epistemology in itself—which would support its non-naive critical systematization, in a coherent way as explained above. Today, this critical reading receives renewed criteria from the considerations of Marxism applied to current sociocultural conditions, for example with authors such as Néstor Kohan (2010), Boaventura de Sousa Santos (2012), Franz Hinkelammert (2006), Edgar Morin and Carlos Jesús Delgado (2017), among others. Reality calls for a perspective that corresponds to its dialectical and complex nature, not just a unilateral, Manichean gaze. It is about overcoming the prevailing positivism that simplifies reality to observe and intervene by compartmentalizing it; it is a completely political strategy within the philosophical realm itself, which encompasses science, especially social and economic science. Positivist thought delays the adequate solution of the contemporary problems of humanity, because it has justified them somehow.

Genuine Dialogue Between Generations

This discourse about the requirements of university education ought to be subscribed by the democratic dialogue among teachers and students, managers and teachers, and managers and students, and among students themselves. The participation of students and student organizations in the collective management bodies of the different levels of principalship—even in the commissions that design the various plans of study in academic departments—makes a lot of sense, so that they are able to take part in important decision-making that has to do with their present and future life. Students generate new spaces for dialogue and debate according to their interests; there are well-known places of discussion such as *The hot corner*[8] at the University of Havana, where students discuss topics or problems of their interest with prominent intellectuals, and even with local or national leaders. At the same time, young people participate in several television programs, in publications such as *Young Cuba* and *Technical Youth*. They are also involved in community cultural options such as *The Art Factory* in Havana, *El Mejunje* in Villa Clara and *El Club Bariay*, among others; in addition to different national and international festivals that they attend both as actors or as audience. *The Hermanos Saiz Brigade* has been a way of encouraging and promoting the work of young writers and artists throughout the country. There are also several mechanisms aimed at promoting new jobs, some of which are especially for young people.

Autonomy and Active Learning

But none of the above would be achieved if students were kept sitting down in the classrooms in front of the teacher listening to the professor and taking notes of what he or she says; this is something that Cuban education has always tried to overcome. Increasing autonomy and active learning are attributes of university education in Cuba, because students, beginning in the first year of their careers, take on tasks of different modalities that ensure their professional participation and their abilities to gain independence and systematic relationship with other professionals in and outside of the university at the same time. Afterwards, this training is sealed with an investigation that supports the degree, or with a state examination, that links the theory with practice in some way. This means that academic activity is embedded in the reality of the country. Such practices are also stimulated by an integral and regular qualitative evaluation of the students that ends with the group analysis of the trajectories of each one and the awarding of a place of employment, to which they are assigned immediately after graduation.

However, those professional activities in the university would not be sufficient if the active construction of knowledge in multiple ways was not stimulated in the classroom; thus, the teacher must know how to decentralize his prominence by distributing it among all the students without losing his role as counselor and advisor. In order to achieve this, he must first master the knowledge of his field and its contextual location from a critical perspective such as the previously discussed; and secondly, to have the necessary pedagogical sensitivity to support the autonomy of his or her students as soon as possible.

The Value of Work–Study

The conservation of the study–work relationship and the perfecting of its fulfillment has been a characteristic of Cuban higher education. This relationship is a central requirement, not only because it prepares the future professional for work, but also because the study–work relationship is carried out in the subjects themselves as a pedagogical principle. In Cuban society, studying and working are the core values around which the national dynamic and the political will of social development revolve. There is a desire for full studying opportunities and full employment in a society, according to international organizations such as the United Nations Economic Commission for Latin America and the Caribbean (ECLAC, 2003).[9] This commission pointed out that Cuba already had 2% unemployment during the economic recovery at that time.

Full Employment and the Needs of Young People

Paying attention to the work needs of young people implies, on the one hand, fostering the development of their social conscience through their professional and political activities both in a curricular and extracurricular manner. On the other hand, it entails the availability of a decent job that allows them to undertake a demanding and thriving professional life, with the satisfaction of important needs such as housing, other material first order needs and spiritual needs of recreation. The needs of further academic formation are guaranteed at no cost by means of the master's and doctoral programs available. As the country recovers economically, the needs of young people should be prioritized even more so that they are able to satisfy all their needs with their professional insertion, a solution that would also alleviate the lives of their closest relatives that in some cases feel obliged to support the young person's financial needs.

The Diversification of Options

As in other times, young people apply for scholarships and receive awards for their social and personal work as students or as specialists, thus complementing their professional, ethical and political training. However, sometimes these opportunities are used as a way to leave the country given the restrictive economic conditions on the island that cannot be denied. Young Cubans face difficulties that are somewhat different from those of young people from other countries who do not have the opportunities to study and work or with the guarantee of medical care; but this is the natural dynamics of the development of human needs and interests: when some needs are met, others of higher order generally arise.

This situation is understandable when young people seek the satisfaction of unresolved needs. However, sometimes they look for consumerism, reject their origins and do not recognize the effort that the country makes to guarantee education, health care and to overcome economic difficulties as well. Although everyone has the right to consider a certain life project and accordingly choose their future, when situations like these occur, there may be something questionable in education or society that did not necessarily work as well as expected. In such cases, an integral reflection of the situation is inexcusable.

Education in general, and particularly university education, should carefully consider requirements such as the ones outlined here, which includes something that is often analyzed in an independent or isolated way: the formation of values, which is emphasized here by critical thinking. All criticality is based on ethical, aesthetic or other values. Any young educated person, but especially one who exercises an intellectual social function, should not ignore these requirements, particularly if he or she has university studies that seek a more acute and committed understanding for the transformation of reality.

Current Obstacles

One of the things that has most affected university education—not only in Cuba—is the formalism of the teaching process and its management, which also extends to research projects on both topics. We cannot allow the fear of institutions to trump the freedom of the student and the critical exercise of creativity behind this problem. Cuban teachers in general have been characterized by a marked interest in the true development of their students and have increasingly emphasized the role of independent study and the autonomy in learning that comes with it.

This phenomenon—of a globalized nature—was accentuated from the moment in which university education began to satisfy the demands of the education transnationals responsible for the accreditation of undergraduate and postgraduate programs in Latin America. This has led to the standardization of educational processes and graduation profiles with the covert purpose of "recruiting the best talent" by core countries in the global north, thus displacing the "developing countries" in certain ways. Until the 1990s, although there were dogmatic teachers everywhere in the world, university education was not subject to these "rigors" of globalization. From its increase, for example, curricular doctorates, with the purpose of producing accurately and regularly an increase in doctorate professionals appeared, which largely ruled out the possibility of programs based on self-preparation. This by no means minimizes the significance of having a considerable number of professionals with doctoral degrees. However, it is the Fordist[10] and forced way to promote graduations, including the theses that are required, to have this industrial-like rhythm in their schedules.

This type of mechanism to achieve high scores and a good international ranking is separating Cuban universities from the real goals set out in the 1961 University Reform, which advocated a more personalized learning process that was not markedly professional; Carlos Rodríguez (1983) emphasized this in his book, *Sharpened Letter*, when he referred to university. Treating the history of universities, and with this, the transit of thought from Bologna[11] to the Porto Alegre Forum,[12] which is said to have started the millennium…from iconoclasm.

As already pointed out, a limitation that may somewhat obscure the efforts and achievements of Cuban university education is the formalization of education, which can be achieved in many ways, such as:

- the weighting of quantity over quality in issues pertaining to the learning process; in other words, the promotion of the student with ignorance of the development of his or her processes of critical reflection, knowledge systematization and creativity. This is related to the teacher's lack of or little zeal for the qualitative aspects of the development of his or her students concerning their cultural and integral development.
- the insufficient exigencies regarding the study of bibliography that implies complexity; also, the substitution of such bibliography by textbooks that simplify knowledge for the sake of a misunderstood simplification of learning. The market for textbooks is imposed on the world, which is worrisome because it castrates the reflective, creative and critical reader. The concern of the enlightened ignorant returns.

The fashion of student evaluation through means that require answers supported by algorithms is integrated to the above mentioned, which leaves aside the possibilities for the display of reflections in essay-type tasks of diverse content, namely theoretical, methodological or practical tasks. This peril looms over Cuban universities that are keen to improve the technical aspects of the teaching process. Knowing how to argue over recognizing correct answers has a substantially greater impact on the integral development of the personality. There is a need for integral development, thinking reservoirs, not one for naive non-professionals or uncritical snobs who are ready to join the fashionable. It takes knowing how to think crosscurrent, and the scenarios found of Cuba demand it. The simplification of knowledge is usually succeeded by the one-sidedness of thought, extremism, Manichaeism.

The avoidance of authentic debate about daily life is present in the academy. However, it is essential to recognize that we do not live in the best possible world and constantly consider how to change it in a consistent and coherent manner based on and through the history and values of Cuban society. Furthermore, any caricature in the study of Cuba's philosophy and history is also due to formalization, something that I have known directly as a higher education official rather than as a teacher. Cuban education, in general, requires taking up this issue continually because it has not yet been solved completely, despite the efforts of those who keep trying.

Institutional administrators and professors, regardless of their age, should value how universities in the last 60 years took the best of each epoch as an example in order to build and sustain a revolutionary position toward reality, not a fashionable one. The snobbishness and the annexationist visions in their different versions push the knowledge of the history of Cuba backwards, so knowing how to identify these positions, however veiled, is a task of reflection for the young person. The existence of different schools of thought in Cuban society cannot be overlooked; some of these ideas are seduced by the advantages of other realities, and/or of certain professional or personal relationships. To be revolutionary does not mean passively coexisting with wrongdoings or merely knowing how to transform; it means working to bring about a transformation to set reality on course from an ethical perspective. To be revolutionary means to turn ethics into action, to exercise a political ethics: the ethics of the common good and of good living.

In these attempts, Cuban education is required to move away from the practiced stereotypes that are common in many of the universities in Latin America that are oriented toward positivist points of view in curricular design, the choice of the bibliography to be studied, the teaching practice and its organization. This point of view disregards the theoretical formation up to a certain extent, for example: ignoring the necessary philosophical and historical framing, ignoring the dialectical perspective in favor of the colonized posture; reducing its role with little dedication to such issues and much less with this ideological sense.

The orientation of higher education from a simplifying behavioral perspective is being sponsored by the European education transnationals, as is the case of Tuning for Latin America (2007), which, under the disguise of exchange and collaboration between universities, aims to standardize the professional training through the learning of competencies. In Cuba, it has brought about some havoc, such as the decrease in the interest for quality in the philosophical formation of the student and consequently of his or her integral formation, tilting the balance in favor of professionalizing education. The above is being oriented toward mechanistic thinking models that tend toward quantification at all costs, based on certain tangible "evidence" structured with an industrialist sense of efficiency.

Educational Experience with Young Cubans

It is interesting to analyze the Cuban programs for the development of young people who have discontinued their studies; such programs have shown good results and therefore may constitute demonstrative references. However, these are not available to be copied because every phenomenon or social process—particularly educational ones—respond to the specific historical and cultural conditions of each country. The value of the Cuban experience lies mainly in the fact that, with few economic resources, changes that favor the development of young people's potential, thus preventing their marginalization from society, have been achieved.

Cuban youth has been studied extensively over the years since the late 1960s, but these studies have intensified since the 1990s, when the economic crisis in the country has worsened to the present day. In this last stage, education has been preserved as a priority within the guidelines for the development of social sciences in the country. Likewise, it serves as a way to monitor the evolution of the situation of young people in terms of study, employment and recreation interests, that seek alternative solutions through specific policies and programs that meet their needs while preserving their social integration (Domínguez, 2015) and have found various ways of implementing them over the years.

Young people's assessments of their situation as individuals or as a generation, their aspirations or expectations, have been intrinsically linked to the economic crisis that was generated in the country in the 1990s. This phenomenon has produced a structural change in Cuban society, generating inequalities and devaluation of education as a means of social mobility for the achievement of a better standard of living. However, the most recent reports confirm that education, along with work, are among the four areas of aspiration of young Cubans (Domínguez, 2015); this suggests that there is a rise in the value young people place on education, as the proposed policies and programs have been taking effect. It is good to point out that in the midst of the country's economic difficulties, the will to prioritize the attention to young people in their social and personal fulfillment is present.

These studies clarify the evolution of young people's assessments of their personal or generational situation. On the other hand, they do not refer to what requisites these educated young people must meet in order to live up to the demands of the time, nor to the conditions university education must meet to achieve such goal. In conditions such as those indicated above, it is crucial to maintain high expectations of the educational and developmental level that young adults achieve. The substantial improvement of personal–professional development, and its corresponding self-effectiveness, open paths to young adults for immediate and future fulfillment and better alternatives for a life project of continuous growth. The best projects have placed culture in the very center of care.

The research carried out at the University of Holguín reveals how it is possible to rescue young people who abandoned their studies for various reasons. The contradictions faced by these young people in terms of their personal and social destiny were resolved in the university with the aid of educational and cultural programs especially designed for them, in which studying was taken on as a form of employment. The investigation practices whose results will subsequently be referred to, modified the pedagogical project that existed at the beginning of the 2000s, especially orienting it to the development of learning self-organization and self-regulation, and therefore to the student's autonomy in the educational process. This change brought about a better orientation of the syllabus toward the integral development of the personality of students, while pursuing their reflection and self-regulation abilities for decision-making in specific scientific and professional tasks, spreading to such intimate-personal level as the temporary organization of family daily activity. The results achieved at the University of Holguín by the researchers Alexander Cordovés (2010) and Deysi García (2010) who directed the investigations of Carlos Manuel Osorio (2009), Rigel Naranjo (2011) and Arledis Díaz (2011), aimed at this same end, are expressed below.

Most of the young adult research participants had not gained access to the university through traditional channels, because they did not meet the necessary admission requirements; this represents the main reason for dropping out of a trajectory in higher education and instead dedicating themselves to other activities or no activity at all. Thanks to the enrollment possibilities offered in the careers of the Municipal University Centers enabled throughout the country, and through the efforts of university professors, experiences like the ones referred to here could be implemented. In the analyses we carried out when the young adults entered the program, we observed the following:

- They paid little attention to the temporal organization of their daily activities. They placed a predominance of attention to family over study. Lifestyles were spontaneous and disorganized without an intention focused on their personal development. That is, they did not favor study as a central activity; instead, they were oriented toward family life.
- Other difficulties in self-regulation were present: especially in the formation of consistent and effective study habits.

The intervention programs created by the authors referred to above significantly favored:

- Awareness of self-organization mechanisms and how to deploy them. This would increase study effectiveness, better academic performance and greater motivation.
- The need to gain independence in thinking and doing in order to meet the demands of the course.

Initially, young people showed low motivation toward studying or learning resources, but intervention programs oriented to self-regulation of learning in the their chosen careers stimulated the development of psychological mechanisms of self-regulation and increased motivation at the same time. These experiences demonstrate the role that guidance plays in these learning processes.

Students with difficulties in their academic performance generally show a lack of motivation to study and toward their development; they maintain passive and evasive attitudes, until education shows them that they are able to take advantage of their development potential. Many of the research participants, as the profession motivated them and opportunities for employment arose, would put aside non-professional activities—even those that paid well—for activities that prepared them to work as professionals. The new motivation for studying allowed the subjective reorganization of their interests.

Clearly, the salary and satisfaction of other needs cannot be underestimated in a young adults' decision-making, but the motivation and the mastery of resources that enable them to achieve quality learning may further generate a positive self-esteem, which is an essential human need. Some of the enrolled students did not finish the program because they would have needed a more specialized program to level themselves up with the group given the extent of their difficulties; nevertheless, several of them looked for other ways to advance their studies and to finish them.

Conclusion

Again, it should be noted that quality university education needs to be founded on considerations and requirements such as those analyzed in this chapter, because this type of preparation enables young adults to make more conscious decisions about life projects that contribute to their development in a social and personal way. As Cuba hopes to achieve a sustainable socioeconomic and cultural development, priorities are placed on health care, study, employment and recreation possibilities for youth. The country has hierarchized attention to young people in a jealous manner, but the policies designed and currently in practice for these purposes are not exempt from the above-indicated risks. This is why it is necessary to collaborate with researchers who devote themselves to study these topics for better insight on new policies and programs that may be proposed in the immediate or medium-term future. However, there is a need to encourage young Cubans to find such incentive in Cuba that they are not enticed to emigrate permanently.

Notes

1. I have done research with Mexican students from the University of La Salle, Bajío, based on the Vygotskian approach on the potentials of development and aimed at fostering the autonomy of young people from the self-organization of learning. This is an indispensable condition for the autonomous and critical construction of knowledge, not only in these ages. Although the problem of education in the youth has been addressed, it is no less true that the preceding levels of education also play a critical role in these developments while they function as preparatory stages.
2. Félix Varela y Morales (born in Havana, Cuba, on November 20, 1788 and died in San Agustín, Florida, United States, on February 25, 1853). Also known as Father Varela, he was a Cuban priest who was also a teacher, writer, philosopher and politician that played an important role in the intellectual, political and religious life of

Cuba during the first half of the XIX century. Father Varela is considered one of the forgers of the Cuban nation.

3. José Cipriano de la Luz y Caballero (born on July 11, 1800 in Havana, Cuba and died on June 22, 1862 in Havana) was a Cuban philosopher and educator. He stood out for his collaborations in science, philosophy and other topics. He is considered one of the people who has done the most for public education in Cuba.
4. Carlos Manuel de Céspedes and López del Castillo (born in Bayamo, Cuba, on April 18, 1819 and died in the Sierra Maestra, Cuba, on February 27, 1874) was a Cuban independence leader. He started the Ten Years War by uprising in arms against the government of Spain on October 10, 1868, and announcing his plan of struggle through the Manifesto of the Revolutionary Board of the Island of Cuba, by granting freedom to his slaves and inviting them to join the anti-colonial struggle. He was Major General of the Cuban Liberator Army and first president of the Republic of Cuba in Arms. He was removed from his post as president in 1873 and afterwards he settled in San Lorenzo, the Sierra Maestra, Cuba, where he died, in 1874, when was caught in an unequal skirmish against the Spanish troops.
5. The fourth generation war is one that holds the central powers of the world today through the media and against countries or people who oppose the capitalist status quo. It pursues the concealment and misrepresentation of the truth through the news (*fake news*) or sometimes very subtle information, which becomes viral intentionally, especially with the current resources of the internet. This news in the mouths of the spokespersons of the United States, their allied countries and those of uneducated and uncritical readers, become truths that are repeatedly asserted without reliable evidence. This mechanism of colonization is not new because it has been tried at different times in history. However, thanks to the circuits that mass media is able to establish, it has gained greater effectiveness today to destabilize or overthrow governments; or in the apprehension of journalists, analysts and other prominent people who do not follow the dictates of the hegemonic power.
6. Telesur is a multi-state news television channel with headquarters in the city of Caracas, Venezuela. It operates under the legal name of Televisión de Sudamérica C.A. It was founded in January

2005 under the jurisdiction of the Ministry of Popular Power for Communication and Information of Venezuela.

7. See Hernández (2015) for more details.
8. It takes the name of *The hot corner* after the group of baseball fans that traditionally meets in the Central Park of Havana, to debate the mistakes of the players that led to defeat in the baseball games during the championship season. It is called *hot* because the arguments are very lively, and it is difficult to walk near the park without overhearing the conversations. The same thing happens in the aforementioned university debates.
9. In English: United Nations Economic Commission for Latin America and the Caribbean (ECLAC or UNECLAC) is a regional organization dedicated to the promotion of economic cooperation In Spanish, it is known as CEPAL.
10. Concept named by Henry Ford and the innovations created around the manufacture and sale of automobiles at the beginning of the twentieth century, Fordism currently refers to the systems and processes used in mass production and consumption.
11. Declaration of Bologna is an agreement signed in 1999 by the Ministries of Education of various European countries (both from the European Union and from other countries such as Russia or Turkey) in the Italian city of Bologna. It was a joint declaration that began a process of convergence aiming at facilitating the exchange of graduates and adapting the content of university studies to social demands, thus improving their quality and competitiveness through greater transparency and a learning process based on the student quantified through the ECTS credits.
12. The World Social Forum (WSF) is an annual meeting held by members of the movement for a different globalization, to organize global campaigns, share and polish the meeting strategies, and so different members of the movement can inform each other of innovations and updates. The International Association for the Assessment of Financial Transactions for Citizen Assistance (ATTAC) and the Workers Party of Brazil (PT) organized the first WSF. It took place from January 25 to 30, 2001 in Porto Alegre, Brazil.

Bibliography

Arias, G. (2005). *La persona en el enfoque histórico culturalista*. Editora Linear B.
Barthes, R. (1973). *El grado cero de la escritura*. Siglo XXI Editores.
Castro, F. (2004). Discurso de clausura. In A. Borón, *Nueva hegemonía mundial*. CLACSO.
Castro, F. (2007). *La historia me absolverá*. Editorial de Ciencias Sociales.
CEPAL. (2003, July 24). *Cuba: evolución económica durante 2002 y perspectivas para 2003* (LC/MEX/566).
Cordovés, A. (2010). *Caracterización de las dinámicas de aprender a aprender en un grupo de estudiantes de Psicología de la SUM Holguín* (unpublished Master's thesis). Universidad de La Habana, Cuba.
de Sousa Santos, B. (2012). *Una epistemología del Sur*. Siglo XXI Editores.
Díaz, A. (2011). *Eficacia del desarrollo y formación profesional: caracterizando un grupo de estudiantes de Psicología* (unpublished Master's thesis). Universidad de Holguín, Cuba.
Domínguez, M. I. (2015). Juventud e investigaciones sociales en Cuba. In J. Hernández, *Antología del pensamiento crítico cubano contemporáneo*. CLACSO.
Eagleton, T. (2018). *¿Por qué Marx tenía razón?* Editorial Ariel.
Fariñas, G. (2006). *Psicología, educación y sociedad*. Editorial Universitaria Félix Varela.
Fariñas, G. (2019). *Aprendizaje y desarrollo humano desde la perspectiva de la complejidad. La teoría en la práctica*. Editorial Universitaria Félix Varela.
Fernández, R. (2000). *Todo Calibán, Obras uno*. Editorial Letras Cubanas.
Freire, P. (2006). *Pedagogía de la autonomía*. Siglo XXI Editores.
García, D. (2010). *Caracterización del estilo de vida en un grupo de estudiantes de Psicología de la SUM Holguín* (unpublished Master's thesis). Universidad de La Habana, Cuba.
Gergen, K. (1992). *El yo saturado. Dilemas de identidad en el mundo contemporáneo*. Paidós.
Guevara, E. (1967). *El socialismo y el hombre en Cuba*. Editora Política.
Hernández, J. (2015). *Antología del pensamiento crítico cubano contemporáneo*. CLACSO.
Hinkelammert, F. (2006). *El sujeto y la ley. El retorno del sujeto reprimido*. Editorial de Ciencias Sociales.
Kohan, N. (2010). *Marx en su tercer mundo*. Editorial Biblos.
Manacorda, M. (1987). *Historia de la educación* (Vol. 2). Siglo XXI Editores.
Marcuse, H. (2016). *El hombre unidimensional*. Editorial Planeta.
Martí, J. (1962). Nuestra América. In *Obras completes* (Vol. 7). Editorial Nacional de Cuba.

Morin, E., & Delgado, C. (2017). *Reinventar la educación. Abrir caminos a la metamorfosis de la humanidad*. Editorial Universidad de La Habana.

Naranjo, R. (2011). *Caracterización de indicadores de reorganización subjetiva en sujetos que han vivenciado una experiencia cercana a la muerte* (unpublished Master's thesis). Universidad de Holguín, Cuba.

Navarro, D. (2006). *Las causas de las cosas*. Editorial Letras Cubanas.

Osorio, C. (2009). *La formación profesional como dirección del proyecto de vida en un grupo de trabajadores sociales que estudian Psicología en la SUM Holguín. Un estudio descriptivo* (unpublished undergraduate thesis). Universidad de Holguín, Cuba.

Pogolotti, G. (2015). *En busca del unicornio*. Ediciones Unión.

Reforma Universitaria. (1961). Archivo Central de la Universidad de La Habana (mimeograph).

Rodríguez, C. (1983). *Letra con filo*. Editorial de Ciencias Sociales.

Rodríguez, R. (2005). *Cuba. La forja de una nación* (Vol. 1). Editorial de Ciencias Sociales.

Siverio, A., & López, J. (1991). *Educa a tu hijo*. Editorial Pueblo y Educación.

Torres, E. (2002). *Félix Varela*. Editorial de Ciencias Sociales.

Torres, E. (2006). *Historia del pensamiento cubano*. Editorial de Ciencias Sociales.

Tuning para Latinoamérica. (2007). *Reflexiones y perspectivas de la educación superior en América Latina*. Universidad de Deusto Publicaciones.

CHAPTER 3

Cultural Violence in Youth?

Marybexy Calcerrada Gutiérrez and Miguel Rojas Gómez

Introduction

The question mark in the title of this chapter is part and parcel of the cultural perspective, a fundamental element of the epistemic character of our analysis herein. Similarly, we attend to the need to ground our discussion in the geographical situation as it relates to physical space. Concretely, linking the urban and the rural is necessary as Cuban reality is marked by developmental asymmetries on the basis of cultural-historical conditions. In order to do this, we employ the concept of cultural offerings, which includes the satisfaction of recreational needs, which attends to the contrasts between urban and public spaces in the Cuban cultural

This chapter was translated by Yoenia Iñiguez Ricardo.

M. Calcerrada Gutiérrez (✉)
Universidad Central de Las Villas, Santa Clara, Cuba

M. R. Gómez
Faculty of Fine Arts, National Pedagogical University of Colombia, Bogotá, Colombia
e-mail: mrojasg@pedagogica.edu.co

R. N. Gioioso et al. (eds.), *Youth and Development in Cuba*,
https://doi.org/10.1007/978-3-030-90866-9_3

reality with regards to development opportunities. This is very important, especially for Cuban youth, because of their pressing needs in the area of recreation.

Likewise, our analyses include gender and race as cultural conditions mediated by relationships of power. These kinds of relationships, in their oppressive sense, are a cardinal axis of violence; in fact, many authors argue that they lie at the heart of violence. This is why research in this field systematizes results that show physical damage, verbal mistreatment and limitations to autonomy and personal development, which are expressions frequently analyzed from a psychological perspective. In determining violent attitudes, we must include other historical and social dimensions that offer broader and more profound explanations, not only visible and obvious manifestations, but also the nature of other destructive conducts that turn out to be more subtle because of their cultural legitimation. The integration of different perspectives to analyze the subjective experience of violence from anthropological, political and other social platforms has been less common than the explanations, usually one-dimensional, that manifestations of explicit damage receive.

Studies of violence have tended to be directed at vulnerable groups based on different criteria—with age and gender being the most common—and researchers have made significant progress on issues like child abuse and violence against women. On the contrary, other generational subjects, like youth for instance, have been given less priority with respect to violence, especially regarding symbolic violence.

The cultural premises taken into account for this critical reflection include traditional practices. We will start our analysis with an examination of pseudo- and authentic culture, which are social-anthropological conceptions that make understanding symbolic violence feasible, which we equate with cultural violence. To analyze the culture of domination, we consider gender and racial evidence fundamentally as exclusionary conditions based on essentialized points of reference that give way to sexisms, racisms and ethnocentrisms. In so doing, we offer appraisals of the concrete behaviors on these indicators by youth in the Cuban context, specifically in Holguín. In sum, this chapter contributes in a reflective way to epistemic indicators for the analysis of violence interpreted through cultural theory, allowing us to better understand expressions of symbolic violence among youth in Holguín. To conclude, we offer useful criteria for the analysis of symbolic violence among youth for other scholars and advocates to use in the future.

Authentic Culture Versus Culture of Domination

Culture is a social-anthropological concept whose meaning adopts its own definition in modern days. Tradition, one of its formulations, has contributed to the displacement of a very important dimension of culture from the ancient world, many centuries before cultural anthropology started to lead cultural analysis. *Paideia* is an ancient notion passed down from classical Greeks, referring to education aimed at human improvement, and it was inherent to the meaning of culture. The German historian Werner Jaeger (2010) reveals that the ascendant idea of the Greek *paideia* is the educational foundation for the development of a truly human character. This idea of "good" spreads in the German *Bildung* (formation) which, as a conception regarding culture, acknowledges a sense of community benefit, as the French Victor Hell (1986) has systematized.

In the modern conception of culture, freedom emerged as an indispensable condition. For example, the teleological moral of Immanuel Kant (1951) summarizes it when he conjugates freedom and culture in his series *Critique*. One of the heirs of his thought, Ernst Cassirer (1993), acknowledged freedom as a central aspect of humanistic values of the German culture.

In this chapter, we focus on the symbolic dimension of culture. Although the classics of the anthropological perspective have correlated certain significance to certain contexts, the greatest clarity in understanding cultural significance belongs to Cassirer himself through his idea of symbol. Known as the pioneer of anthropological philosophy, Cassirer (1993, p. 147) says the following about the symbol: "considering this matter on general terms, it is about determining the 'what' of every cultural form... what function it has." This idea of symbol strikes the ideologies of domination when it offers an alternative explanation of universal conceptions.

Although we do not ignore other aspects of culture as a methodological tool at the end of this part, here we synthetize the criteria we assume as premises for the analysis in question: authentic sociopsychological development based on a distributive justice, freedom in coordination with autonomy and responsibility, and the symbolic dimension inherent to particular contexts.

The so-called pseudo-culture of domination has a long history before the critical theory of Frankfort School[1] explained its pseudo-humanistic character. Other intellectuals have adopted critical reflections of what can be understood as true expressions of culture separated from spurious manifestations. For example, the Brazilian intellectual Darcy Ribeiro (1992, p. 30) classifies these latter as:

> ...corresponding to subdued, dependent societies, therefore, to decisions that are not theirs to make, and whose members are more exposed to cultural alienation, that is to say, adopting as their own a vision of the world and of themselves, that is, essentially, their rulers.

Ribeiro's contribution specifies a type of culture determined by structures of domination. On this matter, representatives of French thought have also carried out important analysis. One of them was Pierre Bourdieu (1977), who stands out on this area.[2] Their harmonized appraisals regarding power and knowledge are a very important hinge when it comes to understanding cultural domination. Habitus, field and capital serve as categorical supports regarding the notion of culture developed by Bourdieu. The first one molds perceptions; the field structures the struggles to gain material and symbolic benefits within different social environments. On the other hand, the possession or lack of capital builds up status and exclusive positions.

The effect of getting a educational degree as an important part of the social status, developed by Bourdieu, has changed in the Cuban context mainly because of changes that have taken place in the Cuban family, among other factors as well. The decades that followed after 1959, the year that marked the political autonomy of the Cuban government, prompted educational policies that ranged from teaching basic literacy to professionalizing competencies for the labor market. This led to a growing interest in getting a degree in higher education in the generations that were born after the 1950s. However, the social imaginary that added prestige to the aspirations characteristic of Cuban youth was negatively affected by the economic crisis the country faced in the last decade of the 20th century.

Bourdieu's categorical apparatus also provides a methodology to understand the referential models of beauty that have been influenced by the racial component since ancient times. His analysis of cultural consumption reveals how the aesthetic coding that individuals systematize is learned in family and school setting and serve as the foundations of their cultural capital. He demonstrates the differentiated consumption of art, which is a symbol of privilege of a powerful elite. This phenomenon turns out to be similar to that of aesthetic consumption in fashion and other *habitus* (to adopt Bourdieu's term) preferred mostly by youth as a symbol of distinction that is considered a privilege of a small group of elites.[3]

Racial Component and Hegemonic Culture: Contributions of Feminism

Here we adopte the contributions of feminism to define the racial component, understanding that, as studies that integrate both perspectives establish, racial and gender conditions are codependent (Collins, 1990). In general terms, the main contribution of black feminism to the racial perspective and its relation to identity has been the absence of the acknowledgment and importance of the black condition itself. On that matter, the Afro-American feminist group *Combahee River Collective* was the first to theorize a policy of identity in the mid-1970s. Before that, *Black skin, white masks,* by Frantz Fanon (1952) had explained the feelings of dependency and inadequacy that black people experience in a white world from a psychoanalytical perspective of colonial relationships. In this foundational work, Fanon relates skin with class; although he does not explain its relationship with gender, he offers a critical analysis of the relationship between race and the choosing of a partner as linked to social identity.

We cannot deny that the emergence of black feminism has been developing for three centuries, however, it was not until recent times that analyses of oppression due to axes like skin color, ethnicity, gender and sexuality have been done. Explanations of indicators of conditions of negative discrimination have been enriched by many black intellectuals and social activists. The North American writer and feminist bell hooks[4] (1989, pp. 42–43) introduced the analysis of skin and class conditions to question the defense of an essentialist female identity that had been so far monolithic. About the identity of black women she stated:

> ...[A] dimension of the oppressor/oppressed, exploiter/exploited relationship is that those who dominate are seen as subjects and those who are dominated objects. As subjects, people have the right to define their own reality, establish their own identities, name their history. As objects, one's reality is defined by others, one's identity created by others, one's history named only in ways that define one's relationship to those who are subject.

Likewise, Barbara Smith (1983), opposing a conception of exclusive identity departing from a white referent and other aspects of domination, supports a theory of simultaneity of oppressions, based on the intertwinement of distinct axes of differences and their resulting forms of oppression. About that North American activist Audre Lorde (1984, p. 116) stated:

> By and large within the women's movement today, white women focus upon their oppression as women and ignore differences of race, sexual preference, class, and age. There is a pretense to a homogeneity of experience covered by the word *sisterhood* that does not in fact exist. (Emphasis in the original)

In the Cuban context, research carried out by historian Carmen Barcia (2015) about the bloody slavery from the transfer of black Africans, shows the devaluation of black women. For instance, obstetrics as a job started in Cuba in the seventeenth century, and records indicate the omission of slaves and black midwives that practiced it illegally because their social stratum, even though they were free, did not allow them to legally certify their practice. The official requirements to get a license to practice this profession included parameters that were not equal for women dedicated to this job, like the certificate of blood cleansing.[5] This class condition, mainly determined by skin color, was even more degrading to these women working as wet nurses. Such experiences show historical aspects of racial devaluation in Cuba.

Nowadays, in Cuba, this old reality has been greatly overcome; however, some experiences show development breaches. Education in Cuba, which is a constitutional right, gives an opportunity to all without any distinction based on race or gender. Nevertheless, statistics corresponding to certain levels of education show disparities regarding such social conditions. Inquiries conducted in the academic year 2010–2011, one of the periods registered in the few bibliographic sources existent on the topic, showed a matriculation in university majors (pedagogical and medical majors are not included) distributed among white, black and mixed race of 57%, 14.2% and 29% respectively. Something similar happened with the faculty: White, 71%; black, 11%; mulattos, 18% (Pérez et al., 2013).

Researchers on this topic who stand out, like Yulexis Almeida Junco (2015), contribute to the cultural explanation of the access of black and mixed race population to Cuban higher education, in which we can notice a sub-representation of this part of the population in the university environment. Among others, the psychologist Mayra Espina (2008) has systematized results that show superior white presence in management positions, as well as an over-representation of black and mixed race population in more vulnerable housing conditions that plays a role in limiting a rise in social status. As Espina (2017) states, there is still a lack of intersectional research that relates racial and gender perspectives; research in this tradition in Cuba, specifically, is limited.

To supersede the euro-referenced hegemonic model, historian Wania Sant'Ana (1995, p. 75) states: "Educators should also devote themselves to the task of making common not only a universe of colors, sounds, words and meanings, but also the different types of hair, noses and lips." That is to say, it is essential to culturally integrate the racial condition of other aesthetic expressions that have traditionally been guided by hegemonic and exclusionary concepts of beauty.

Pseudo-Culture in the Interference of Relationships of Gender

In this analysis we depart from the binary organization that characterizes Western thought, where men represent the one and women the other. Relationships of power-subordination between men and women give a political dimension to this kind of bond. Feminist thought has contributed to the analysis of this topic with its respective thesis of equality.

Patriarchy, correlated to the unequal distribution of public and private spaces and the division of jobs based on gender, is the way of organizing society that creates inferior opportunities and access for women and superior opportunities and access for men. The historical-theoretical treatment given to patriarchy comes mainly from feminism. The British philosopher from the eighteenth century, Mary Wollstonecraft (1994), stands out for her work *A Vindication of the Rights of Woman,* which mainly focused on the unequal influence that educational contexts exert on men and women. Another equally important contribution in the 18th century that followed was the work of English suffragette John Stuart Mill (2008), especially in *The Subjection of Women.*

A work of great relevance from the 19th century for the understanding of family as a determinant of gender inequality is Friedrich Engels' (2006)

The Origen of Family, Private Property and the State, which highlights the oppression of women by men. The support for Marxist foundations about the forms of capitalist production was based, undoubtedly, on the premises of this analysis. Engels makes an analogy between the classist structure of bourgeois society and the sexist structure of family. However, Marxist oriented feminists in the late 20th century, like anthropologist Gayle Rubin (1996) with her work *The Traffic in Women: Notes on the 'Political Economy' of Sex,* are the ones that have made visible in a more explicit way the relationship between the surplus generation and the domestic economy. They explain that the reproduction of the workforce, in which generally women participate without any economic gain, is related to the surplus nexus of the daily relationship between men and women. In fact, a very important contribution of the Marxist wing of feminism was to incorporate class as an axis of domination between the sexes that also includes men.

The division of work based on gender and the hierarchy between public and private spaces are important dimensions of the analysis of patriarchal organization. *The Human Condition* by Hannah Arendt (1974) offers a broad reference about the division of work and its relation to private and public spaces departing from the practices in ancient and modern city-states. More contemporary authors like sociologist Soledad Murillo (2006) have deepen their understanding about certain aspects of what constitutes the private and the public, particularly related to domesticity. This Spanish feminist elucidates what domestic means as an attitude, i.e., when an individual does not perceive herself in a self-reflective way, and, on the contrary, is always attentive to meet other people's emotional and material needs. According to Murillo, self-reflection is an aspect of identity that is replaced by their dedication to others, which places a woman in a subordinate relationship. Expressions of the hierarchical structuration between the public and the private as the differential space between women's traditional condition and hegemonic masculinity are the family and the labor market, just to mention two.

The previous theoretical analysis and the reports of expressions of inequality between men and women throughout history, which have been adopted here as a logical-thematic explanation, support patriarchy as a domination system mainly based on the political economy that structures the relationship between the sexes. However, despite this important statement, the argumentation of control mechanisms that bring about female subordination, with some exceptions, lacks work that can directly link the culture of domination to the formation of exclusive gender identity.

The important Marxist premises and the analysis carried out by its followers, feminists of oppression, enrich the analysis of the basis of domination, but they do not lead this field toward the definition of identity. In Kate Millett's (1975) *Sexual Politics*, for instance, the author emphasizes the unequal exercise of power resulting in inequality for the sexes; but, even though she deals with the essentialized improvement of identities, the cultural aspect is included in a sense of what is intrinsic of each gender. Although she does point to culture as a condition of change for identities, she does not explain how gender identities can be fairly reorganized from culture.

All this theoretical tradition points to a reorganization of relationships between the sexes, and, in several cases, is implicitly or directly included a political economy and a sexist education, including family. But there is limited explicit reference to the normative-legal system as a cultural context that holds and can favor the reversion of the unequal order between the sexes. It means that the cultural aspect is more visible in tradition than analyzed by the contexts that make up that tradition and that would come together in what is authentically cultural headed toward a development with no exclusions.

On the other hand, patriarchy has not only implied the domination of men over women, but in the wide range of relationships among men and women themselves there are also other forms of hierarchical differences that imply ways of exclusions as well. These are evident in articulation with class and ethnic relationships mainly, as shown in the contributions of Marxist feminism, black feminism and masculinity studies. About the latter, Michael Kauffman (1994) systematizes the relationship between power and any manifestation of masculinity. The Canadian sociologist explains the contradictory experiences of power that men face based on the interaction of class, ethnicity, and other identity axes that alienate and oppress.

Epistemic Criteria to Understand Violence from a Cultural Perspective

So far, we have presented theoretical contributions about cultural dimensions relevant to the determination or the overcoming of violence. However, the links between violence and the foundations of those dimensions, like hegemonic culture that leads to discrimination based on race and gender have not always been explained enough. We propose the following cultural criteria to understand violence:

- Pseudo-cultural traditions that split culture's authentically constituent principles; specifically referring to freedom, in correspondence with autonomy and solidarity. Likewise, the conception of common good. In the same way, an ethical-legal tradition defined by distributive relationships and an anthropological conception of recognition of individual and group differences.
- The historical configuration of contemptible identities establishing as referent an abstract universal conception of identity constituent of essentialized and contrasted identities.
- The conception of exclusive identities as support of colonizing organizations fulfilled in dividing racial practices. Inequalities structured in a history of devaluation of the non-white subject like his objectification as subject of satisfaction and desire, either sexual or in another pragmatic sense. Likewise, the configuration of aesthetic otherness that has given way to a culture of resistance as autonomy has increased.
- Gender, as a condition that hierarchically classifies human relationships, is an unequal constituent order of the modern-colonial world that has had its origin in a long history of feminine devaluation. Consequently, the domination system called patriarchy is a multiform mechanism evident in all social and cultural structures that has aimed at achieving sustainability in a binary system of organization of the world. For that purpose, it has made use of control mechanisms like the legal system, education in its broadest significance, among others. Such organization has determined rigid hierarchies, essentialisms and justification of sexisms that turn a patriarchic culture into an expression of a hegemonic-pseudo-culture of domination.

Experiences of *Cultural* Violence Among Young Adults in Holguín

With the purpose of analyzing how the above theoretical frameworks apply to the realities of youth in Cuba, we draw from empirical information of several works as well as our own survey research conducted with a group of young people in Holguín. For this, 25 youth were interviewed, representatives of young university students in the area. Students of Psychology and Singing Majors at the University of Holguín and the University of Arts,[6] respectively, were sources of information about contents that in the first part of this work are presented as cultural conditions traditionally mediated by relationships of power; for instance, the geographical situation like urban and rural spaces and the racial and gender significance as developmental conditions. Interviewees' perceptions regarding the availability of cultural offerings, an important need of human development, especially in youth, were included, as well as their levels of satisfaction regarding the availability and quality of recreational activities. Although the central topic of this text is not youth psychology as a stage of development, in order to understand the analysis here presented we need to take into account certain characteristics of the subjectivity of this period of life and its social context. For the purpose of this analysis, the social situation of Cuban youth takes on special significance, which includes, among other aspects, interest in partner selection and certain kinds of needs like recreational, aesthetic and financial, which become prominent demands in this stage of life. Psychosocially speaking, Cuban youth have not regularly systematized the ideal level of maturity (i.e., autonomy from a Cultural-Historical approach) to meet their most pressing developmental needs, which further frames our analysis below.

Within our sample, Psychology majors focus part of their academic curriculum on the social analysis of development. In the case of the University of Arts, students' professional formation is characterized by encouraging cultural consumption. The sample contained 9 male and 16 female interviewees, a difference that represents the gender gap existent in majors, like Psychology and the performing arts.

Cultural Offerings in Rural and Urban Spaces: Authentic Culture or Hegemonic Culture in the Shaping of Identity Patterns in Young People?

The integration of the appraisals delivered by the interviewees and other sources of research systematize important differences in the developmental conditions between the rural and the urban context. Concretely, the data collected reveal limitations regarding access to different kinds of opportunities for youth living in rural areas, for instance, the difficulty of accessing certain majors at institutions of higher learning in the province, particularly the most specialized ones in the performing arts. Likewise, there is a limited network of services and facilities in these areas, which makes it necessary to travel to other cities to meet developmental needs, not only to study, but also to access technological development, which is part of the cultural context. At the same time, respondents emphasized the existence of major transportation difficulties to meet those needs. Cultural deprivation in rural areas in Cuba is determined by the country's economic limitations, despite the inclusive efforts by the Cuban state to democratize access to education and culture through national policies.

In Cuban rural areas, there is a lack of sociocultural programs. There is not only the need for a material infrastructure to support the development of a system of cultural activities, but also the need for the traditions of those places to be included, e.g., craftworks, music, dance, games of rural folklore. Furthermore, local products of the rural culture that are frequently used for their market value for foreign visitors need to be preserved and promoted for appreciation by and within the local population. For that reason, it is necessary to re-value the symbolic dimension of what is autochthonous in the face of the globalization of foreign expressions that have been structured as culturally dominant. The Cuban social imaginary regarding rural population disqualifies aesthetic patterns and the cultural capital characteristic of these contexts, which stimulates in the rural population a search for an identity based on urban patterns, in other words, a manifestation of spurious identities.

The dominance of urban patterns, like aesthetic models that include clothing and its correspondent accessories, has a strongest influence in the youth, especially during the first years of this period, since psychological maturity is not shaped and conduct is motivated by extrinsic factors. In other words, since there is not an optimal development of autonomy, a very important part of psychic development with repercussions in the self-esteem, there is more vulnerability of adopting as their own alien referents just because they are dominant.

At the same time, this is a sensitive period for the selection of a long-term romantic partner, a process that, along with the configuration of identity based on the relationship between the expressions of authentic culture and culture of domination through their link with the urban and the rural, surfaces as extremely important in our research. In this respect, urban men, affected by patriarchal organization as a condition of domination based on the intertwinement of different axes—sexuality, skin color, class, geographic location—turn out to be most in demand. As such, male youth in the Cuban context tend to imitate a hegemonic identity, characterized by young people living in urban areas with their aesthetic patterns and cultural capital. In other words, it is a tendency of assimilation departing from the dominant model, in which local, rural aspects of identity are left out because they are deemed to have less value and appeal. Consequently, that model of relationship in which cultural minorities are led by expressions of hegemonic identity is an expression of culture of domination.

Recreational Needs: Satisfaction from Abstract Universal Patterns or Concrete Situated Preferences?

When asked about their satisfaction regarding the quantity and quality of cultural offerings, the absence of cultural-spiritual[7] opportunities stood out prominently. Among the suggestions given by the interviewees was the increase of the availability of dramatic plays and musicals and their diffusion. The interviewees critically highlighted that there is little correspondence between the economic situation of youth and the cost of those offerings, i.e., they are too expensive. Some respondents also stated that there was little correspondence between the activities offered and the diverse preferences and tastes of local youth. They criticized the presence ofactivities designed to cater to the preferences of the majority—for instance, a popular music genre like reggaeton—in the absence of activities for those with other particular preferences. Interestingly, many participants pointed out that the comedic plays that do get produced in Holguín usually satirize people living in rural areas, black people and other secondary expressions of identity.

Thus, the data we collected from young adults in Holguín reveal that neither the quantity nor the quality of cultural offerings in the area are satisfactory. Concretely, the design of cultural offerings suffers from informed awareness of and attention to the diverse interests of the youth in Holguín. There is, in fact, a lack of public studies that inform cultural programming based on situated local perspectives. This insight is also based on interviews we performed with the people in charge of the cultural sector in the territory. Despite the limitations we have identified, the demand for cultural-spiritual activities like those mentioned above over other activities that require even larger budgets turned out to be significant in Holguín.

The Role of Race in Cultural Violence

Cuban social policies are very solid regarding overcoming all kinds of discriminations. Therefore, the expressions of racial discrimination are subtle, but still important; they are, in short, a reproduction of historical stereotypes. In the case of Holguín, there are specific demographic characteristics of colonial and post-colonial history that influence racial perceptions.[8] The stamp of the Spanish colony was more evident in this part of the country, which makes Holguín a province with a notable majoritarian white population descended from European settlers. This demographic datum was acknowledged by all the interviewees as an explanation for the majoritarian presence of white people in developmental scenarios like the university.

In another sense, the interviewees acknowledged the presence of negative stigmas regarding the black population; these stereotypes emerge in times of conflict, like during arguments. In such cases, respondents identified expressions traditionally used to devalue black Cubans as mechanisms of conflict between black and white people. Disdainful manifestations like criticizing physical traits that are characteristics of this population and are not considered to be aesthetic are also very common. Explanations that integrate several axes of discrimination stand out, for instance, those that combine place of origin (rural or countryside), family education (uncultured), economic situation (poor). These data converge with perspectives emphasize the configuration of identities and its hierarchical structures from the intersection of different sociocultural variables. As such, it is not surprising that research participants clarified that such prejudicial expressions do not homogenously characterize all Cuban contexts. For example, such manifestations are not usually present in multicultural urban settings and university scenarios that tend to integrate differences, which is an expression of authentic culture. In more traditional contexts, we find a prevalence of prejudices and defamatory remarks, expressions of a culture of domination.

Our data reveal that regarding the racial component as a condition for equality, historical discriminations have not yet been overcome. The demographic bias imposed by the Spanish stamp lays a curtain before isolated and underlying manifestations that are still present. Obviously, the solid social policies in Cuba directed to erase all kinds of discrimination have contributed to the eradication of the biggest differences. However, the ones that have a cultural nature, the less obvious ones, are harder to overthrow. In this sense, we identified among the interviewees the significant allusion to sports and popular dancing as vocations of the non-white population, which would serve as an explanation of their reduced presence in higher education.

It is true that the sports sector has gained great prestige for the country; however, sports (e.g., being a professional athlete) as an axis of identity does not have the same status as other activities, e.g., doctors, university professors, among others. We found a similar result when discussing dancing, which holds a certain connotation of sensuality and association with mixed-race or black Cubans. In short, we consider such ideas as reproductions of social stereotypes.

Gender: Expression of Relationships of Symbolic Power or Condition of Social Development?

Regarding gender, our respondents did not acknowledge the existence of discrimination. Instead, they made reference to the formal discourse that has been characteristic of Cuban social policies that encourage women's development. Although there is no visible awareness of gender inequality, the previous appraisals hide the unequal relationships found through other sources of information.

Studies about the behavior of patriarchal organization in the Cuban context prove the existence of this phenomenon. Research carried out by Cuban psychologist Norma Vasallo (2005) in women of different generations shows variations in the generation of women that was born during the Special Period, i.e., the Cuban economic crisis of the 1990s. There are two visible tendencies in the latter group; one groups demonstrates the desire, following in their mothers' legacies, to orient themselves toward professional formation as a guarantor of insertion into economic life and toward personal realization. This involves postponing maternity, a characteristic present in Cuban women that were born from 1959 on). The other tendency shows those whose expectations in life surround marriage, which will help them satisfy their vital material needs.

This latter tendency represents a step backward in the formation of a transcendent identity that was one of the main achievements of gender relationships in the Cuban context after the Cuban revolution. It also relates to work done by researchers like Natividad Guerrero (2011), who has pointed out there there are complex dynamics in relationships that can and do decrease gender equality in contemporary Cuba.

The university women who participated in our study have chosen professional formation as one of their main developmental goals. This is in correspondence with ideal of progress of Cuban women, despite inequalities deeply rooted in patriarchy that characterize some dynamics and relationships. These include the reproduction of historical inequalities within couples relationships and a family organization in which a woman is financially dependent on her husband. Likewise, there is an overload of domestic work on wives and female heads of household.

The behavior of these parameters is more complex in rural areas. The data we gathered coincide with those of the last Population and Housing Census of 2012, which indicates that the main sources of employment for rural women are in the agricultural sector: 24% in Basic Units of Cooperative Production,[9] 16% in farming and livestock cooperatives, 12% associated to credit and services ooperatives and as farmers. There is less than 1% connected to mercantile companies, and only 13% working as free lancers in different sectors (ONEI, 2012).

Moreover, census data reveal that most rural women do not go beyond their historical socioeconomic conditions. 56% of rural women are housewives, and they tend to base their feminine identities on the domestic sphere. Research by researcher Blanca Munster (2017) shows that the overload of roles in this area, along with the demands and limitations of rural contexts leave little time for the well-being and personal and professional development of women. The youth that were interviewed for the analysis presented here live in urban areas, and, although they acknowledge the deprivations present in rural areas, they cannot criticize the impact of those deprivation on gender condition. Gender inequalities in this context, although marked, are not visible for the common perception of people who are not affected by them; they hide behind the omnipresent ideology of gender equality. In this sense, they reproduce homogeneous models that hide those differences and constitute patterns of domination.

The conditions that keep these women from achieving higher levels of autonomy include patriarchal organization and the absence or limited existence of social services to support their greater independence. Women living in rural areas frequently dedicate themselves to unpaid labor (in the home) and dedicate a lot of time taking care of others (also unpaid). In that sense, there is no legal or material support (like daycare) to facilitate, through services offered by governmental institutions, the distribution of those functions to achieve a better use of the women's private time.

Conclusion

Here we offer a *final synthesis* about referential criteria for the analysis of symbolic violence in the youth, as well as regarding the regularities found on this matter in the youth who participated in our research from Holguín. In so doing, we hope to equip the reader with criteria that, in the cultural order, give them epistemological tools for the analysis of symbolic violence in the youth.

Criteria of Symbolic Violence in Youth

Conceiving youth as a collective subject from an abstract universal referent makes contextual differences invisible. The totalizing perspective the springs from the hegemonic pattern leads to conditions of dissatisfaction and exclusionary development. To have the same orientation and access to the consumption of cultural goods, vocational profiles, among other experiences that gain relevance in youth as a period of definition, gives way to discriminatory practices based on a framework of power, cultural conditions, among others, and territorial spaces belonging to minorities.

The different foci that characterize cultures of domination concretize a binary organization between essentialized identities, excluding those that do not fit. Racism, sexism and ethnocentrism, which bolster such ways of thinking and acting, are obstacles for the realization of certain dimensions and needs in youth. Among these dimensions we find sexuality with its correspondent expression and aesthetic and love relationships (couple-hood), among others.

Conceptions of domination that, justified in structures of authority like the age criterion, take away creativity and autonomy, which are central processes and formations in youth. This brings about generational violence, structured in parameters regarding responsibility, capacity for critical judgment, among other maturity indicators.

Symbolic Violence Among Youth in Holguín

The design of cultural offerings prioritizes the preferences of a segment of the youth from Holguín in correspondence with urban patterns. This design tends to satisfy popular aesthetic needs, like in the case of the music reggaeton. Simultaneously, the cultural preferences of those who are exceptions tend to be left out. In other words, they become a powerless minority, meaning that in a structure of cultural domination (pseudo-culture), their recreational needs or their authentic traditions, like in the case of rural contexts, are left out or rejected.

Although the once-existent cultural devaluation of Black African influence in Cuba has been overcome at an institutional level, youth acknowledged that there still are prejudices and discrimination in the social subjectivity. Devaluations are based on traditional preconceptions that reproduce expressions of cultural domination. However, such pejorative attitudes do not have the same incidence among youth for they show certain assimilation and preference for aesthetic patterns characteristic of the black population, like the natural form of their hair. Likewise, our research of youth cultural violence in youth in Holguín offers a systemic understanding that integrates economic conditions, family education and geographic location to explain the limited opportunities of development available to black people, including youth.

Youth reproduce a speech of gender equality characteristic of Cuban and other international contexts. However, in our sample of youth, we did not find critical opinions on the many subtle differences (e.g., in perceptions of athletes and of popular dance music) that are part of cultural preconceptions that limit meeting of developmental needs of the local population. In this sense, especially in the rural context, we detect the prevalence of traditional hegemonic gender hierarchies as they relate to the attribution of housework to women and maternity as a symbol of feminine identity. Experiences conditioned by traditions have systematized the separation between domestic and public spaces, which continue to lead to the confinement of a reproductive life especially for women. These tendencies keep them from meeting their cultural needs.

Notes

1. The Frankfurt School was a group of intellectuals and researchers influenced by the thoughts of Georg Hegel, Karl Marx and Sigmund Freud, which emerged in the first half of the twentieth century. It was aimed at criticizing the social–historical conditions in which the previous theories were formulated.
2. See also the work of Michael Foucault (1992), Bourdieu's contemporary.
3. See also Bourdieu (1997, 1998).

4. Written in lower case letter because of the self-identification of this North American writer and feminism activist with subaltern positions.
5. Blood cleansing is a certificate that proves that the holder has a status equivalent to those considered pure, in this case, white European. That is, it is a legitimation of what was socially acceptable at the time, based on patterns that were structured in relationships of symbolic power from which black people were excluded. This certificate was required to practice certain professions in Cuba during colonial times.
6. The University of the Arts was previously known as the Higher Institute of the Arts, founded by the Cuban government in 1976 in Havana.
7. The cultural-spiritual dimension refers to the significance of superior needs, that is, those that extend beyond survival, e.g., food and shelter. It is comprised of the recreational, educational, aesthetic and professional growth and affiliation.
8. This is the explanation of the racial component of society in Holguín agreed on by consensus. Unlike other territories, there was no significant settlements of black slaves. Holguín as a city dates to the early 1500s composed of Spanish settlements for commercial purposes, absent the conditions for the development of human exploitation in the racial domain. This does not mean, however, that there is no stamp of blackness in the social imaginary.
9. Center of labor production, which belongs to the sector not budgeted by the Cuban state, aimed at the generation of goods and services through the cooperative participation of groups of workers. This type of production is common in rural areas, especially in farming and livestock activities.

Bibliography

Almeida, J. (2015). Educación superior, raza y política social. Una breve reflexión desde Cuba. In P. Vommaro & V. Labrea (Eds.), *Juventud, participación y desarrollo social en América Latina y el Caribe* (pp. 125–137). Escuela Regional Most-UNESCO Brasil.

Arendt, H. (1974). *La Condición Humana*. Editorial Seix Barral.

Barcia, M. (2015). *Oficios de mujeres, parteras, nodrizas y "amigas": Servicios públicos en espacios privados (Siglo XVII–Siglo XIX)*. Editorial Oriente.
Bourdieu, P. (1977). Sur le pouvoir symbolique. *Annales, 32*(3), 405–411.
Bourdieu, P. (1996, December 9). Los motivos de la Ira. *Der Spiegel* 50.
Bourdieu, P. (1997). *Capital Cultural, Escuela y Espacio Social*. Siglo XXI Editores.
Bourdieu, P. (1998). *La distinción. Criterio y bases sociales del gusto*. Editorial Taurus.
Cassirer, E. (1993). *Las ciencias de la cultura* (6th ed.). Fondo de Cultura Económica.
Collins, P. (1990). *Black feminist thought, knowledge, consciousness, and the politics of empowerment*. Unwin Hyman.
Engels, F. (2006). *El origen de la familia, la propiedad y el Estado*. Fundación Federico Engels.
Espina, M. (2008). Viejas y nuevas desigualdades en Cuba. Ambivalencias y perspectivas de la reestratificación social. *Nueva Sociedad, 216*, 133–149.
Espina, M. (2017, June 26). Por un socialismo donde el conocimiento se vuelva política. *Temas*.
Fanon, F. (1952). *Piel negra, máscaras blancas*. Éditions du Seuil.
Foucault, M. (1992). *Microfísica del poder*. Las colisiones de Piquete.
Guerrero, N. (2011, April 15). *Cuba: Inequidad de género resiste puertas adentro*. Inter Press Service, Cuba. http://www.ipsnoticias.net
Hell, V. (1986). *La idea de cultura*. Fondo de Cultura Económica.
hooks, b. (1989). *Talking back: Thinking feminist, thinking black*. South End Press.
Jaeger, W. (2010). *Paideia. Los ideales de la cultura griega* (Vol. II). Editorial de Ciencias Sociales.
Kant, E. (1951). Crítica del juicio. In E. Kant, *Crítica de la razón práctica. Crítica del juicio y Fundamentación de la metafísica de las costumbres*. Editorial El Ateneo.
Kauffman, M. (1994). Men, feminism, and men's contradictory experiences of power. In H. Brod & M. Kaufman (Eds.), *Theorizing masculinities* (pp. 142–165). Sage.
Lorde, A. (1984). *Sister outsider: Essays and speeches*. The Crossing Press.
Millett, K. (1975). *Política sexual*. Editorial Aguilar.
Munster, B. (2017). La sostenibilidad de los emprendimientos solidarios de mujeres: los desafíos para las políticas públicas. *Revista Economía y Desarrollo, 158*(1), 91–105.
Murillo, S. (2006). *El mito de la vida privada: de la entrega al tiempo propio*. Siglo XXI Editores.
ONEI: Oficina Nacional de Estadística e Información. (2012). http://www.onei.gob.cu

Ortner, S. (1979). ¿Es la mujer con respecto al hombre lo que la naturaleza a la cultura? In O. Harris & K. Young (Eds.), *Antropología y Feminismo* (pp. 12–21). Editorial Anagrama.

Pérez, B., Almeida, A., & Bajos, E. (2013). Equidad en la Educación Superior Cubana: Logros y Desafíos. *Revista Lusófona De Educação, 24*, 117–133.

Ribeiro, D. (1992). *Las Américas y la civilización. Proceso de formación y causas del desarrollo desigual de los pueblos americanos*. Editorial Casa de las Américas.

Rubin, G. (1996). El tráfico de mujeres: Notas sobre la "economía política" del sexo. In M. Lamas (Ed.), *El género: la construcción cultural de la diferencia sexual* (pp. 35–96). PUEG/Editorial Porrúa.

Sant'Anna, W. (1995). Hacia una percepción de género y raza. *Revista Especial/Fempress.*

Smith, B. (Ed.). (1983). *Home girls: A black feminist anthology*. Kitchen Table: Women of Color.

Stuart, J. (2008). *La Sujección Femenina*. Artemisa Ediciones.

Vasallo, N. (2005). Género e identidades en tránsito. Cubanas en diferentes contextos sociales. *Informes psicológicos*, No. 7 Medellín - Colombia. Ene-Dic. p. 11–27.

Wollstonecraft, M. (1994). *Vindicación de los derechos de la Mujer*. Ediciones Cátedra.

CHAPTER 4

Espacios que pesan/Heavy Spaces: (Re)thinking Rural Youth Through Gender and Generation

Ania Pupo Vega

Introduction

Rural spaces have always been the focus of my interest, (re)configuring theoretical positions and moving my practices to increasingly center the

This chapter was translated by Doralkis Ramírez Ronda.
I draw some of the ideas in this essay from the final paper in my Agriculture and Rurality course in the Postgraduate Program in Political Sociology at the Federal University of Santa Catarina (UFSC) in Brazil. I use the same title inspired by the book of the well-known American feminist Judith Butler (1993), entitled in Portuguese *Corpos que pesam: sobre os limites discursivos do "sexo."* In the Portuguese language, "pesam" is translated into "to matter/to be important." In the text, however, I try to place/play with its meanings in Spanish and English: heavy, as in annoying, hard, violent, hard to bear.

A. P. Vega (✉)
Universidade Federal de Santa Catarina (UFSC), Florianopolis, Brazil

R. N. Gioioso et al. (eds.), *Youth and Development in Cuba*,
https://doi.org/10.1007/978-3-030-90866-9_4

narratives of those who live in them. In these discourses, I have discovered the power of the category of space as a social marker, allowing me to perform analyses that problematize a pluralistic and tremendously complex reality.

Through my research experiences in eastern Cuba, various issues have drawn and maintained my attention, among them: the denial of peasant origins; the existence of preconceptions about people who live in the countryside, labeling them as old fashioned, *guajiros*[1]; the increase of emigration to urban and suburban areas, and the related tendency to interpret these migration strategies as an indicator of success, especially for younger people, and to link the possibility of returning home to failure. In this essay, I reflect on issues related to the rural environment that may mark the above-mentioned experiences, namely the ways in which people perceive themselves in contexts of rurality, influenced by relations of power and hierarchies instituted through the design of policies where the rural is placed in disadvantaged positions.

The relationship between ways of perceiving and experiencing spaces and their (im)permanence is interesting. In this sense, young people design and implement strategies to achieve their goals in life according to how they understand that their contexts/territories offer (or not) real opportunities to successfully do so. Delving into current debates about rurality and the existence of links between academic and/or political discourses and the practices that occur in these relationships is a legitimate concern that reveals multiple approaches and ruptures. We find dialogues that reflect tensions between those who problematize and question the realities from the academy and those who decide on the implementation of actions to transform or perfect such realities. Finally, processes and relationships occur in spaces, and as such, incorporating space in academic perspectives provides diverse nuances that allow for deeper and multidimensional analysis. In sum, social phenomena occur in space–time relationships, and thus, their dynamics change according to their historical, social and cultural character.

In tackling gender relations in rural contexts, I take into account the weight that space adds to inequality gaps. Employing an intersectional[2] approach allows me to place space within other social markers that, in addition to gender, gain relevance in interdisciplinary research. Variables such as age, schooling, gender, economic status, sexual orientation, skin color, among others, are intertwined.

The academy in Cuba has scarcely addressed rural areas. The gap is greater in those of eastern Cuba, where its provinces historically show the lowest Human Development Indexes (HDI) in the country, with figures that are below the national average. In 2015, the Cuban Human Development Index (HDI) measured 0.82, surpassing the results for the eastern provinces: Granma (0.71), Las Tunas (0.75), Holguín (0.76), Santiago of Cuba (0.77) and Guantanamo (0.78).[3] These are important data, though they fail to show the complex economic and socio-political realities of the country revealed through other less tangible aspects of life.[4] In addition, by reflecting the mean values, interesting analysis of their extremes are blurred.

If academic attention to rural areas has been absent, young people, who are considered key actors for rural development, have also been understudied. Population aging,[5] signaled as an alarming phenomenon in Cuba, is presented as a critical situation for rural areas particularly in the eastern region. These figures have not triggered actions beyond the descriptive lists of "what to do" without deepening and contextualizing the "how to do it."

Using the above as my point of departure, in this essay, I intertwine threads to weave together the relationships between the categories of space (focusing on rurality) and youth. I place the category of space in a central position because of the analytical force it bears, particularly for understanding the elements of the context that are (dis)configured as "old spaces" and determine the exodus of young people. The value that rural spaces have for economic dynamics challenges the implementation of policies that are capable of transforming them (from the perceptions, representations and narratives of their populations) into living and working spaces.[6]

It is in such categories, understood as social constructions, where I will place the focus of my reflections. These categories are being constituted based on my relations with the spaces that I inhabit and inhabit me in return: urban, academic, feminine and feminist. I try to carefully weave these threads together so as not to get caught in them.

Methodology

In this chapter, I mention some of the results obtained in research project carried out in rural communities in the municipalities of Cacocum and Calixto García, in the province of Holguín. The methodological body of these projects has privileged the qualitative paradigm and the ethnographic method aimed at querying and interpreting the realities from the narratives of their protagonists, in order to minimize the risk of academic construction. I seek to fracture traditionally dominant forms of scientific knowledge and theoretical and methodological presuppositions characterized by androcentrism and blind to gender inequalities. Qualitative data pursue comparative and illustrative purposes.

Discourse analysis was central. Focus groups were formed in communities intentionally to foster the equitable participation of both men and women, different age groups (predominantly young people) and different occupations and sectors (agriculture, public health, education, sports and homemakers). Participant observation, semi-structured group and individual interviews and group techniques were used to collect information.

Choosing Threads

The categories of space, place, territory and landscape are gaining importance in scientific thought, as their uniqueness and usefulness become clearer. According to Ovidio Delgado (2003), the concept of space has been permanently reconstituted and redefined according to the demands of the processes of knowledge production. Nevertheless, Edward Soja (1993) emphasizes that although we might consider space primarily as a given, we must recognize its organization and meaning as products of a social experience. Therefore, the incorporation of space as a geographical support in social scientific analysis is key, as pointed out by Francisco Alburquerque (1995) regarding the examination of socioeconomic activities.

These references of space as social construction are inspiring. In Cuba, Mayra Espina (2001) maintains that the rescue or reinforcement of territoriality in social scientific studies and in the design of policies is based on the relevance of the mid- and micro-levels of the reproduction of social relations. In this line of thought, Luisita Iñiguez (2002) speaks of space-territories, considering them as a social product, a support for life in society and, at the same time, a conditioner of human projects. She also places space as a symbolic, affective and political reference. Thiago Nogueira de Queiroz (2014) builds on the work of Milton Santos[7] to clarify the differences between the concepts of landscape, space and territorial configuration, claiming that landscape is only the visible part of the territorial configuration, a material system and relatively immutable, while space conveys the value system and is permanently transformed.

Important contributions to the conceptions of space are due to feminist thinking, which advocates for looking beyond its materiality and highlighting its cultural and subjective dimensions by introducing the public and private elements and the category of power. In this context, Teresita De Barbieri (1993) takes the gender system as a power system that influences the ways in which power is structured and exercised in different spaces. Furthermore, Doreen Massey (1994) elucidates how space and gender are mutually constructed, with deep intersections and reciprocal influences.

I now turn to a discussion of *lo rural*, rurality.

Basting Rurality

The categories of urban and rural are yet another binomial as seen through the historical tendency of the West to eschew their links and instead focusing on asymmetries, inequalities and privileged priorities: urban–rural, culture-nature, male–female, reason-emotion, modern-traditional, development-underdevelopment, among many others. These binomials have invaded and provided criteria for academic and political discourses and have become a rule of thumb and common sense. Their limits, however, are usually so rigid that they hinder the existence of porosities and hybridizations and creating these classifications has become an obsession for those in positions of power. According to Zygmunt Bauman (1999: 75):

> To classify consists of acts of inclusion and exclusion. Each act of designation divides the world into two: entities that correspond to the name and the rest that does not. Certain entities can be included in a class - made into a class - only in the same proportion in which other entities are excluded, separated. Invariably, such an operation of inclusion/exclusion is an act of violence perpetrated on the world and requires the support of a certain coercion.

This reflection allows us to understand how categories that involve nature, emotion, feminine, rural, traditional have been marginalized or excluded from analysis, when compared to their robust "opposites": society, reason, masculine, urban, modern, etc. And, in practice, it is common to find the strong hegemonic presence of the subject-male-urban-rational-modern-among other markers (white, young, professional, heterosexual) and increasingly exclusive classifiers, not only of people, but also of spaces (in its various scales) that would be typecast as rural, old-fashioned, marginal, peripheral, with their corresponding negative connotations.

Iván Illich (1996: 167) places the conceptions of development from a critical perspective as follows:

> ...development can be imagined as a gust of wind that pushes people out of their place, out of their family space and places them on an artificial platform, in a new structure of life. In order to survive on this exposed and elevated base, people are compelled to reach new minimum levels of consumption...

Thus, we must critically analyze visions of rural development expressed in urban language. Put another way, rurality has been examined based upon a belief that it is unable to name and explain itself, and thus the language of its more powerful "opposite"—urbanity—must be used to bring it into being, making it visible, nameable.

The traditional and reductionist visions of rural development defended the productivist approach that established nexi between the rural and the potential of the agricultural sector, which prevented valuing these spaces as potential places for plural functions within territorial dynamics. The approach of *new rurality*[8] overcomes these limitations by presenting the rural as a geographical, economic and social space where its population performs multiple functions beyond those related to work on the land.

For William Vergara (2011), rural development models were characterized by the search for economic growth as a way to overcome poverty and a state of backwardness, but his vision was restricted to agricultural productivity and ignored the multifunctionality and complexity of rural lifestyles. The author criticized the economistic vision, typical of development models, as alienating to the extent that it subordinates the dimensions of human life under the different forms of capital, e.g., human capital, natural capital or social capital.

One of the consequences of such visions of development has been deruralization,[9] that is, the loss of the "typical" customs and lifestyles of rural spaces.[10] Another consequence is the territorialization[11] of inequalities insofar as development prioritizes/privileges some individuals and groups over others. The territorially differentiated effects of development in Cuba surfaced in studies assessing the effects of the economic crisis of the Special Period of the 1990s and the economic reforms that have been implemented since. Espina (2001) demonstrated, for example, that the negative impacts tend to be concentrated in the eastern part of the country and further deepen the historically accumulated disadvantages of that region (Espina, 2001).

Youth(s)

The definition of the category of youth(s) entails profound complexity due to the moment it marks in human existence. I intend (not innocently, I might add) to highlight the plurality, as a provocation added to the elements of that complexity. Youth is a transitory stage that supports important aspects of life. Difficulties in its definition add up the multiple psychological, biological and sociological dimensions of this stage and the multiple ways in which these dimensions interrelate.

Although research on rural youth abounds in Latin American academies, debates have not focused on the definition of the category; different theoretical positions are utilized as the basis upon which to study specific research questions. To assume a definition of the category of rural youth rests upon what is understood as rural and as youth, both of which are triggers of corresponding debates both in academic and political fields. It also demands a careful attention to the cultural, symbolic, social and political references that involve these categories and, therefore, revitalize the definitions of categories under construction. Quoting Stropassolas[12] (2002: 131), "theoretically addressing youth represents a challenge, to the extent that this sociologically problematic category is considered."

The Economic Commission for Latin America and the Caribbean (ECLAC, 1993: 3–5) of the United Nations defined youth, especially in rural areas, as the stage of the life cycle that is most characterized by strategic thinking, and in which many of the most decisive decisions and actions of a life strategy are taken. This is in contrast to childhood, when the future is a cause for fantasy, while in the successive phases of full adult life, irreversible decisions already made and increasingly disappearing options make the development of life strategies progressively lose validity as the life cycle is completed. Strategies developed by rural youth are essentially oriented toward individual goals, even if they are carried out in association with other people and despite young people's contribution to the reproduction of their family household.

In a report[13] on the state of research about rural youth in Latin America, Gabriel Kessler (2006: 7) presented elements that define rural youth as:

> Young people whose lives develop in the rural world, inhabiting country areas or adjacent towns, whether or not they involve themselves in rural activities. As for the geographical limits, those villages where up to 2,000 inhabitants live, although there are some stances that include young people of rural origin who inhabit the urban peripheries and hold up to 5,000 inhabitants. As for age group, a consensus exists to include 15 to 24 years old; other stances advocate contemplating a greater range of ages between 13 and 29 years old.

From another stance, Kummer and Colognese (2013) define rural youth beyond the framework of residence in rural contexts. The authors take into account the life experiences young people have within that context, their participation in a productive family unit where they occupy culturally defined spaces. They argue that the subject relates to a specific way of being, which is linked to a reality in which the world of work and the world of life merge and become confused. They emphasize that rural youth are not reduced to this condition; they are not hostages of a space or situation, but articulators of life practices like any other.

This definition refers to aspects of rural youth that are related to identity and way of life, which causes me to focus on the specificities of the context. Social phenomena are localized, and it is essential for the understanding of their expressions, as well as their causes and possible outcomes. The analysis of poverty, gender violence, inequalities, for example, evoke the necessary articulation with contextual approaches.

Interweaving Threads

The way in which processes and relationships occur involves contexts, whether to facilitate or hinder such processes, to make them more complex or simplify them. They undeniably provide nuance; ruralities compromise that nuance. Social phenomena occur in certain contexts and times; their projections would not be the same in different times and spaces. To portray the panorama of the disadvantages that rural contexts and emigration have historically accumulated, I present the following statement expressed in the mid-1990s (in terms of alarm) that maintains a sad validity that has become provocation:

> Rural areas today only house half of those who were born there in the sixties. Insufficient attention has been given to this reality, which translates, among other things, into problems of poor preparation and difficulties of adaptation of those who migrate (Dirven, 1995, p. 123).

In the quote, Martine Dirven (1995, 2003, 2016) refers to population aging in the sending zones and its consequences, and she emphasizes the neglect of young people who wish to remain in rural areas. She warns about the need of taking advantage of their potential and their necessary inclusion in the political life of their native localities, and she analyzes how living conditions in the agricultural sector have made little progress, which prompts youth to leave in pursuit of a better future outside the agriculture sector.[14]

Covering the complexity that the category of rurality involves is a permanent challenge for the social sciences. Rural youth is not a monolithic group (as no human group is); there is no unique profile of rural youth, although the association with being old-fashioned, inferior, and less developed remain carved in social imaginaries along with the agricultural activities and other stereotypical dynamics that take place in rural spaces. It is urgent to examine the perceptions and representations that young people have about their rural contexts. What are their projections, strategies and expectations concerning the conditions in which they develop their lives? Rural youth, perceived as social actors whose participation in the economic, social and political dynamics of their spaces, are decisive, as is in the real participation in the public management of their localities.

The unique relationships established by young people with their spaces define their decisions to leave or remain in their rural contexts. Thus, it is essential to know the circumstances in which they implement these strategies, what their main motivations are to emigrate, and what resources they use to achieve their goals. Do they envision their migration as permanent or temporary, and are their decisions voluntary or forced due to their inability to mobilize appropriate financial and relational resources to stay? Which spaces do they occupy at home, are they constant or do they insert themselves into new spaces, and if so, why and how? It is imperative to examine the structural conditions that configure opportunities and obstacles to find a place to stay and belong. These investigations demand a gender perspective that fractures the traditional look of research and reveals the inequalities that constrain the freedom of women and men, in diverse expressions and magnitudes.[15]

Cuba in the Skein

Academic studies on youth in Cuba are not vast. Such emptiness is even deeper in relation to rural youth in the eastern part of the island. In a 2017 essay on rural studies in Cuba, María de los Ángeles Arias and Arisbel Leyva (2017) refer to studies on youth within the topics that are beginning to be identified together with the strategies of agricultural producers to face the crisis of social participation, environmental issues, the masculinization of rural spaces, gender violence in these contexts, rural poverty, among others. In the tour that the authors take through pre-revolutionary rural studies and those subsequent to the political and social change of 1959, the category does not appear to have been the object of any rigorous academic studies.

We find a definition of youth in Cuba, assumed by María Isabel Domínguez (2003: 6) after recognizing the complexities involved in the category, which includes[16]:

> ...people between 14 and 30 years old, because we estimate that the processes described above take place during that age range and because youth policies cover that interval. However, we take into account that between these ages there are notable biological, psychological, and social differences. Therefore, for my studies I have distinguished the presence of three subgroups, whose central core, where typically youthful processes are expressed, is precisely the intermediate segment.

There is wide acknowledgement of the urgency to investigate the particularities of the rural population in research about youth. Author Adriana Elías (2017: 112) points out:

> ...of the analysis whose object of study is the population residing in rural areas, those focusing on young people are very scarce, which shows the lack of interest in knowing and recognizing their concerns, expectations, needs, levels of participation and identity traits, among others.

According to 2012 figures, the Cuban population between 15 and 29 years old in rural areas represented 21.5% of the rural population as a whole, 26% of Cuban youth in general and 4.8% of the total population. In 2017, these figures decreased. Rural youth represented 19.97% of the rural population, 23.37% of Cuban youth and only 4.59% of the total population of the country, according to data from the National Bureau of Statistics and Information of Cuba (ONEI, 2018). It is worrisome that the figures of the rural youth population continue to decrease, if we think about the replenishment and/or expansion of the labor force for the performance of agricultural activities and for the multiple ways that these spaces impact the country. It is important to note that young people in the eastern provinces represent more than half of the country's youth (51.56%) and rural youth (51.62%) in particular (ONEI, 2018).

Trends reflect migration toward cities, a phenomenon that has attracted much attention. We can refer back to Arias' (1993) study, in which he analyzes emigrations,[17] with emphasis on the eastern region, as a consequence of the technological-organizational model based on large state property and on the patterns of the Green Revolution. Another noticeable phenomenon is the tendency to masculinize rural areas. In my own research carried out in rural areas of Holguín, I have verified masculinized contexts, which reinforce a pattern in all the provinces of the country, that exhibit a higher Masculinity Index in rural areas compared to urban areas. In 2017, there were 1,155 males per 1,000 females in rural areas, according to ONEI data (2018).[18]

My research[19] in rural areas of Holguín that has developed from a socio-environmental perspective since 2003, and the studies of poverty from a gender perspective carried out in the last ten years, allow me to talk about some characteristic aspects of such spaces that are placed in the narratives of men and women who live in them. Hereinafter, I examine the most significant ones or, at least, those that I consider most revealing.

The perceptions of agricultural work held by rural inhabitants of the communities I have studied involve material and symbolic values. In the narratives, the monetary dimension associated with work is contemplated, although it has an important place-based link to other employment options (formal or not) regardless of educational level. Generally speaking, work in the fields is considered "poorly valued, brutalizing and exhausting," while other characteristics are the "uncertainty" about the results of the crops as they are subject to climatic variables, epidemics and other factors "beyond their reach."

Socialization in the context reinforces behaviors and values that respond to a culture with strong patriarchal nuances that distinguish it from other spaces.[20] This culture shapes the sexual division of labor from which different roles and jobs are assumed for women and men, with different "weights,"[21] the least heavy assigned to women and the heaviest for men. These classifications are deconstructed in the daily dynamics in which women assume agricultural and domestic tasks simultaneously regardless of the effort required for their completion.

Access to education, universal and free in the Cuban context, is marked by the precariousness of some of its institutions. Often in school, rural contexts are not sufficiently valued; urban life is used as a benchmark and indicator of success. Furthermore, the study of professions disconnected from the dynamics of rural contexts is also encouraged. Cities represent opportunities for contact with other access points[22] and cultural references, as well as health, leisure and technological services.

Narratives within the framework of a participatory rural gender diagnosis,[23] developed in the communities of Maceo, in Cacocum, revealed that people feel discriminated against for: being young and having no experience; being of rural origins because of the negative connotations attributed to this identity and its connection to the perception of scarce and deteriorated material resources; their ways of dressing; personal and family economic precariousness that does not allow adequate satisfaction of basic needs. Other discrimination issues dealt with gender, sexual preferences and religious practices. This young-rural-poor triad (for both genders) is lacerating in their daily lives.

A gender perspective is intended as a category holding a strong analytical potential that also becomes a political tool (Louro, 1997: 21) and enlightens about inequalities and their possible mitigation from different levels of action. In my research, women point out that there are few sources of employment locally, considering that they disregard those related to agriculture or livestock. These are perceptions that respond to ways of thinking about social relationships, proper to space, which have been incorporated and re-produced in their points of reference. This vision has a direct negative impact in relation to women's performance and places them in disadvantaged situations, reducing opportunities that favor employment and training opportunities.

There are also cultural factors linked to greater instability of women at work. For example, one of them is related to the notion that women are responsible for other people (dependents) and the responsibility to perform non-paid jobs, often considered as "help" even by the women themselves because of the naturalization of cultural patterns in the rural setting. In that sense, complex domestic dynamics overload women because of the wide variety of tasks they carry out. Such duties because of the absence, in the rural context, of services that favor caring for dependent people and/or in the extreme ages of life. Available time for women to take advantage of opportunities and carry out paid jobs and participate in other community and social events is conditioned by these dynamics. Women, for the most part, perceive domestic work as "repetitive, endless and exhausting," and "is not valued even by the family itself."

Another factor that weaves the relationships between work and women together is linked to the ways in which jobs are structured. Women hold subordinate positions with lower income than those of men, located in directive and direct production structures, a particularity that responds to the employment of women, generally, in positions that do not require high educational or skill qualifications (but not to different remuneration for performing equal duties). It is likely that the positions assigned to women are those of kitchen assistants (head cooks are usually men), secretaries and cleaning assistants, thus reproducing the activities that are culturally considered as "feminine or typical of women." As such, employment is constituted as an extension of the domestic responsibilities that women perform in their daily dynamics.

Emigration is another phenomenon that stands out in rural areas studied, understood as a strategy undertaken by young women. Women had better resources for their reintegration into new spaces, generally in the urban periphery. In their motivations, they place the intention of not reproducing the poverty experienced by previous generations, namely parents and grandparents, who support the youngest people to leave their native rural spaces due to the reduced possibilities of economic development and well-being that they offer. Among the main reasons for moving to urban spaces, they refer to: the pursuit of a higher quality of life quality and a greater spectrum of opportunities away from agricultural activities and rural spaces, which includes improvements in mobility, food, training opportunities, recreation and access to cultural consumption.

Imagined Threads

The ways in which people project their future lives in a given space speak of conformity and pleasure in it. When asked how they view their communities in the coming years, the non-verbal expressions of strangeness confirmed that they had not considered the matter, at least with any level of elaboration; in most people; such contexts are not thought about for the long-term future. The answers generally focused on the word "worse," and "need to improve." Both responses convey a comparative element stating that the current situation is not the desired one and that it could even get worse in the coming years.

When given the task of making a drawing of their community in the future, it was interesting to see (in the communities of Cacocum) the illustration the "Antonio Maceo" Sugar Mill as an essential element for the community, which tells us about the desired projection of retaking the past.[24] The temporal dimension does not move toward the future; it is identified and wished for, with a reference of a former state of well-being and prosperity in the locality from decades past.

From this same line of analysis, the scarce elaborations of life projects split in two ways in relation to remaining or not. Some families have decided to stay after considering their age as a hindrance to insertion into new contexts and their own permanence as support for those who migrate (sons and daughters). Such arguments are based on medium age and older adults who, as an act bordering on the stoic, state: "I am staying because I have no other choice, but I will do everything to get my children out of here." This "out of here" marks a feeling of being trapped that also tells us about how they think of, feel and live their rurality.

Found Threads

Young women represent the largest number of people who emigrate from the communities I studied. In their new spaces, they commercialize their traditional roles, which is impossible in their places of origin. Among the most demanded ones are food processing posts (sometimes linked to self-employment), maids, live in care giving, etc.; such work is in demand in the absence or insufficiency of these services in urban centers and aids women who migrate in their integration into paid work.

In the narratives of both men and women, they emphasize that they come from conditions of disadvantage and inequality when they arrive in the new spaces (generally inhabiting urban periphery or rural–urban areas), and hence they are stigmatized. In short, rural origins are negatively represented in the social imaginary that reproduces the country-city dichotomies. Rural migrants, with their cultural and identity patterns, mix and hybridize with those they acquire in their new daily dynamics.

Unfinished Threads

Spaces do not embrace, in themselves, "heaviness" and "lightness"; these are conditions that are being constructed in the multiple intersections of their social, historical, cultural and political subjective dimensions. These constructions cross and shape the physical and symbolic representations that are formed about rural spaces and from which valuable information is obtained to reconsider and project policies.

Casting a look at these realities from a gender perspective allows understanding differentiated ways of perceiving and experiencing spaces for both men and women. They are, in this way, pieces of information that could bring about the proposal of affirmative actions for vulnerable groups where women (in general) and young people are always represented. The lack of public policies with a focus on rural youth[25] as well as policies of a generational and gender perspective is evident.

Migrations to urban spaces continue to compromise socio-demographic and economic dynamics, in both rural and urban settings. The referenced studies on rural spaces confirmed the existence of negative perceptions about those contexts associated with work in the field (both productive and reproductive), limitations, disadvantages, discrimination and deprivation, which contribute to the conformation of this "heaviness" experienced by the people who inhabit such spaces and who, in different ways, compel younger people to leave them.

The "heaviness/importance" that rural contexts have in the social and economic life of the country has not translated into visions, policies and public management that make them appealing to rural youth, who perceiveonly the "weight/burden" of their precariousness. The academy is constituted as an indispensable space to make this "heaviness" visible.

Notes

1. The word has its origins in the Spanish-American War of the late nineteenth century, where the peasants of Cuba and Puerto Rico

were called to fight the Spanish empire, for their independence, allied with US troops who called the peasants "war-hero" (war hero) and was deformed over the years to: wař-hiroh, warjiro, guajiro, goajiro, guajiro, etc. However, there are other possible origins of the term. It is used pejoratively to refer to people living in rural areas, in the countryside. An English equivalent would be "country bumpkin."

2. Intersectionality is an analytical tool to study, understand and respond to the ways in which gender interacts with other identities and how these interactions contribute to unique experiences of oppression and privilege. Therefore, it is an indispensable methodology for work in the fields of development and human rights. See Intersectionality: A Tool for Gender and Economic Justice. Association for Women's Rights in Development (AWID), August 2004. Available at: https://www.awid.org.
3. The United Nations Development Program (UNDP) collects data and publishes national rankings every year. See www.hdr.undp.org/en. For subnational statistics, see the Statistical Yearbook of Cuba produced by the National Bureau of Statistics and Information (ONEI) of Cuba at www.onei.gob.cu. For a recent discussion of the eastern provinces, see Feinberg (2019).
4. Based on indicators of access to health and education, which are universal and free in the Cuban context. Nevertheless, these statistics do not reveal the precariousness of these critical services in rural areas. Furthermore, they overlap with problems related to the salaries of state workers, which contribute to impoverishment and social inequalities because they are too low to cover basic needs.
5. Oliveros (2010: 139) asserts that the aging of the Cuban population, especially in rural areas, has become an important problem. See Blet (2010) and research by the Center for Demographic Studies of the University of Havana.
6. See Wanderley (2009) for a thorough reflection on this matter.
7. Milton Santos, a Brazilian geographer, refers to the studies of space as opaque and bright. I draw from his work and apply opacity to rural spaces.
8. In the early 1990s, in some Latin American academic media, the notion of new rurality was proposed as an umbrella concept capable of identifying "new" phenomena and processes and, in some cases, to update previously existing approaches to studying the rural

world. Others argued that the emergence of a new paradigm of rurality would make previous approaches obsolete in the social sciences in the current period of global restructuring (Grammont, 2004). One of the main criticisms put forth against the new rurality is its scarce theoretical development.

9. Wallerstein (2001: 1–2) reflects on what he considers the three main structural pressures on the economy-capitalist world: the consequence of the process of denaturalization of the world, which is now very advanced; the long-term consequence of cost outsourcing, which has led to ecological exhaustion; and the process of growth of democratization in the world. The combination of these three pressures would create a huge structural reduction, in the long term, of the profits derived from production, to the point of transforming the capitalist system into an unprofitable system for the capitalists themselves.
10. Bustillos (as cited in Matijasevic & Ruiz, 2013: 29) underlines how despite the changes in the rural world of Latin American countries in the last fifty years, there is a coexistence between the traditional and the modern, with a strong presence of the peasant and indigenous modes of production; this perspective attempts to overcome the vision of rural populations as passive consumers of urban styles, recognizing the coexistence of different ways of life.
11. Espina (2001) references the circumstances in Cuba that determine the growing importance of the local-territorial in socioeconomic transformations: trends of spatial selectivity and differentiation are being revealed as a consequence of the crisis of the 1990s that made it impossible to continue the equalization policies among the different regions in Cuba. Opportunities for access to material and spiritual well-being and the economic reforms that have been implemented rely on links with the globalized economy that necessarily include activities and competitive spaces and capital attractors. Meanwhile, others fall outside that realm of possibilities, as reform entails higher degrees of business and territorial decentralization, and there is no clear and coherent plan for territorial development centered on the potentials of local actors and participatory horizontality between urban spaces and rural spaces.
12. Translated from Portuguese by the author.
13. This is an exhaustive analysis based on 68 sources, 52 Latin American and 16 from other parts of the world.

14. Martine Dirven served as head of the Agricultural Development Unit of the Economic Commission for Latin America and the Caribbean (abbreviated as CEPAL in Spanish or ECLAC in English) at the United Nations and then as an independent consultant. In her article, quoted in the text, the author reflects on the common expectations that rural youth have—almost without exceptions—to find a better future outside agricultural activity. He emphasizes that, in the seminars on agricultural development, the growth of the sector, productivity, innovation and modernization were of interest, without taking much care of the population's desires.
15. On rural youth in Brazil, see Weisheimer (2005).
16. The National Bureau of Statistics and Information (ONEI) of Cuba includes three groups: 15–19; 20–24 and 25–29 that approach those contemplated by the author.
17. The author refers to "the insufficient valuation of agricultural work and the lack of expectations offered by rural communities, to a population that increased their levels of culture and education year after year, made urban centers their main attractions, giving rise to a true process of 'de-scaling' reflected in negative migratory balances, in which the eastern region, especially its mountainous areas, suffered the greatest losses" (Arias, 1993: 65).
18. For further consultation, see M. Á. Arias (1993).
19. See Pupo (2013, 2015, 2017) and Pupo and Martínez (2015).
20. To address gender violence in the relationship between couples and the strong links between their expressions and rural, mountainous and coastal spaces, see Hernández (2014).
21. Paulilo reflects extensively on these aspects in Brazilian contexts in a classic article for Latin American Rural Sociology. See Paulilo (1987).
22. See Pupo (2014).
23. Pupo et al. (2011).
24. A broader description of the impacts on the subjectivities of the closure of the "Antonio Maceo" Sugar Mill can be found in my article *Change, then do I exist?* (in the process of publication). Similar results were obtained in research carried out on active citizen participation, coordinated by Virginia Hardy Casado of the University of Holguín and the Félix Varela Center in the Matamoros community of the Consejo Popular Edecio Pérez,

in response to the local demand to envision the future of the community
25. In Brazil, there is the National Program for Strengthening Family Farming (Pronaf), which could be an interesting reference.

Bibliography

Alburquerque, F. (1995). *Espacio, territorio y desarrollo económico local*. CEPAL.

Arias, M. Á. (1993). *Cambios fundamentales en la estructura interna de los obreros agrícolas después del triunfo de la Revolución. La clase obrera agrícola en la región oriental* (unpublished doctoral dissertation). Universidad de La Habana, Cuba.

Arias, M. Á., & Leyva, A. (2017). Los estudios rurales en Cuba. Reflexiones sobre la estructura social y los cambios en la agenda de investigación. *Revista Universidad de La Habana, 283*, 243–258.

Bauman, Z. (1999). *Modernidade e Ambivalência* (M. Penchel, Trans.). Jorge Zahar Editor.

Blet, A. O. (2010). Dinámica reciente del proceso de envejecimiento de la población rural en Cuba. *Novedades en Población, 6*(11).

Butler, J. (1993). *Bodies that matter: On the discursive limits of 'sex.'* Routledge.

CEPAL: Comisión Económica para América Latina y el Caribe. (1993). Estrategias de vida de los jóvenes rurales en América Latina. Obstáculos, condicionantes y políticas. LC/R.1307 (Sem. 73/3), Santiago de Chile.

De Barbieri, T. (1993). Sobre la categoría género. una introducción teórico-metodológica. *Debates en Sociología* (PUCP), *18*, 154–169.

Delgado, O. (2003). *Debates sobre el espacio de la geografía contemporánea*. Editorial Universidad Nacional de Colombia.

Dirven, M. (2003). Algunos datos y reflexiones en torno al rejuvenecimiento de la población en los territorios rurales. In P. Tejo (Ed.), *Mercados de tierras agrícolas en América Latina y el Caribe: una realidad incompleta*. CEPAL.

Dirven, M. (2016). *Juventud rural y empleo decente en América Latina*. FAO.

Dirven, M. (1995). Expectativas de la juventud y el desarrollo rural. *Revista De La CEPAL, 55*, 123–138.

Domínguez, M. I. (2003). Juventud cubana y participación social: desafíos de una nueva época. Retos y transformaciones. In *La sociedad cubana. Retos y transformaciones* (pp. 1–38). CIPS.

Economic Comission for Latin American and Caribbean (ECLAC). (1993). Estrategias de vida de los jóvenes rurales en Amércia Latina. *Obstáculos, condicionantes y políticas*. Santiago de Chile: CEPAL.

Elías, A. (2017). Juventudes rurales en la Cuba contemporánea. *Estudios Latinoamericanos* (UNAM), *39*, 99–116.

Espina, M. (2001). *Territorialización de las desigualdades y desarrollo local. Reflexiones a partir de la reforma económica cubana* (conference paper). ONGs, Gobernancia y Desarrollo en América Latina y el Caribe, Montevideo, Uruguay.

Feinberg, R. E. (2019). *Cuba's forgotten Eastern provinces: Testing regime resiliency*. Brookings.

Grammont, H. C. (2004). La nueva ruralidad en América Latina. *Revista Mexicana de Sociología, 66*, 279–300. https://doi.org/10.2307/3541454

Hernández, Y. (2014). *Lecturas culturales sobre la violencia contra la mujer en la relación de pareja. El caso de estudio Moa* (unpublished doctoral thesis). Universidad de Oriente, Cuba.

Illich, I. (1996). *Necesidades*. In W. Sachs (Ed.), *Diccionario del desarrollo. Una guía del conocimiento como poder* (pp. 167–175). PRATEC.

Iñiguez, L. (2002). Precedencias y efectos de los procesos de la década del 90 en las desigualdades sociales en Cuba. *Anales de Geografía de la Univ. Complutense, 22*, 157–185.

Kessler, G. (2006). La investigación social sobre juventud rural en América Latina. Estado de la cuestión de un campo en conformación. *Revista Colombiana de Educación, 51*, 16–39.

Kummer, R., & Colognese, S. A. (2013). Juventude rural no Brasil: entre ficar e partir. *Tempo da Ciência, 20*(39), 201–220.

Louro, G. (1997). *Gênero, sexualidade e educação: uma perspectiva pós-estruturalista*. Editora Vozes.

Massey, D. (1994). *Space, place and gender*. Polity.

Matijasevic, M. T., & Ruiz, A. (2013). La construcción social de lo rural. *Revista Latinoamericana de Metodología de la Investigación Social, 5*, 24–41.

Nogueira de Queiroz, T. A. (2014). Espaço geográfico, território usado e lugar: ensaio sobre o pensamento de Milton Santos. *Para Onde!?* (UFRGS), *8*(2), 154–161.

Oliveros, A. (2010). Los cambios cuantitativos de la población rural en Cuba. *Novedades de Población, 6*(11), 113–151.

ONEI: Oficina Nacional de Estadísticas e Información. (2018). Anuario Demográfico de Cuba, January–December 2017. http://www.onei.gob.cu

Paulilo, M. I. (1987). O Peso do Trabalho Leve. *Ciência Hoje* (UFSC), *28*.

Pupo, A., Martínez, T., & Laso, E. (2011). *Diagnóstico participativo. La experiencia en la comunidad de Maceo (Holguín, Cuba)*. Hegoa, Instituto de Estudios sobre Desarrollo y Cooperación Internacional del País Vasco. ISBN 978-84-89916-62-3.

Pupo, A. (2013). Una mirada a la pobreza desde el género. Caso de estudio: Monte Alto. *Ciências Sociais Aplicadas* (UEPG), *21*(2), 151–160.

Pupo, A., & Martínez, T. (2015). *Violencia y pobreza: un acercamiento desde lo vivencial* (conference paper). X Congreso Iberoamericano de Pensamiento, Holguín, Cuba. ISBN: 978-959-255-147-3.

Pupo, A. (2015). *Pobres mujeres pobres* (Conference paper). VI Conferencia Científica Internacional, Universidad de Holguín, Cuba. ISBN: 978-959-16-2138-2.

Pupo, A. (2017). Pobreza en el oriente cubano: lecturas desde las perspectivas de género y espacio. In A. Leyva & D. Echavarria (Eds.), *Políticas públicas y procesos rurales en Cuba: aproximaciones desde las ciencias sociales* (pp. 228–251). Ruth Casa Editorial.

Pupo, A. (2014). The impact of globalization on subjectivities in Cuba: A gender perspective. *International Review of Psychiatry, 26*(5), 589–594. https://doi.org/10.3109/09540261.2014.917612

Soja, E. W. (1993). *Geografias pós-modernas: a reafirmação do espaço na teoria social* (V. Ribeiro, Trans.). Jorge Zahar Editor.

Stropassolas, V. L. (2002). *O Mundo Rural no Horizonte dos Jovens* (unpublished doctoral dissertation). Universidade Federal de Santa Catalina, Brazil.

Vergara, W. (2011). Desarrollo del subdesarrollo o nueva ruralidad para Colombia. Cartografías del desarrollo rural. *Revista de la Universidad de La Salle, 55*, 33–66.

Wallerstein, I. (2001). *Capitalismo histórico e civilização capitalista.* Rio de Janeiro: Editora Contraponto.

Wanderley, M. N. B. (2009). *O mundo rural como espaço de vida: reflexões sobre apropriedade da terra, agricultura familiar e ruralidade.* Editora da UFRGS.

Weisheimer, N. (2005). *Juventudes Rurais: mapa de estudos recentes.* MDA.

CHAPTER 5

Studies *about/with* Youth: Methodological Dialogues for Practices of Science with Life

Deysi E. García Rodríguez and Alexander A. Cordovés Santiesteban

(Un)Adjusting Frames

The dialogues we propose here have been "under construction" in a constellation of collective spaces we have walked during the last 16 years. They are the result of a *participative mindset* that has required us to place ourselves in relation *with* our own actions—our teaching and research practices, relationships—and *with* the outcomes of those actions—research results, lessons learned, pupils and mentees, other relationships. This *participative mindset* is an act of empathy—that is, as the understanding of our duty in a relationship in which the participants have the same conditions,[1] it implies responsible participation, a dialogic relationship where identification with others is possible and, fundamentally,

This chapter was translated by Yoenia Iñiguez Ricardo.

D. E. García Rodríguez · A. A. Cordovés Santiesteban (✉)
Universidad Internacional Iberoamericana, Campeche, México

R. N. Gioioso et al. (eds.), *Youth and Development in Cuba*,
https://doi.org/10.1007/978-3-030-90866-9_5

the creation of something new (Bakhtin, 2012 [1924]). It has allowed us to open ourselves up to other people's experiences, dialogue, exchange meanings, identify ourselves and create something new, which did not exist before the act of empathy. And as it happens, in the relationships that constitute and, at the same time, are constituted in these collective spaces, new ways of practicing, teaching and learning are created (Cordovés, 2017). Meanings are (re)created, (in)visibilities are revealed and new possibilities emerge that question our ways of relating, learning, thinking and thinking about ourselves, perceiving spaces, times and relationships as flows in evolution, communication and updating through different directions (García, 2018). In those relationships we have learned that:

> There is no such thing as the first or the last word, and there are no boundaries for dialogical context; it climbs to an infinite past and an equally infinite future. Past meanings generated in the dialogue of previous centuries can never be stable, concluded once and for all, finished. They will always change, renewing themselves in the process development of those dialogues. (Bakhtin, 1999, pp. 292–293)

Taking this point of reference into account, in this chapter we have two principal goals. First, we will present a theoretical-methodological systematization of the research projects we have done or supervised *about* youth, identifying what we consider to be their main potentialities and limitations and analyzing them from other possible perspectives in the area of research *with* youth. Then, based on that analysis, we will discuss those indicators that we have found to be effective for this kind of scientific practice *with* youth. Throughout this article, we dialogue with contributions from the social sciences and humanities that facilitate our historical and cultural understanding of studies *about/with* youth, highlighting the possibilities of creating flexible methodologies.

We consider it necessary to define and problematize the notion of *framing* that we will use throughout the chapter. The understanding of framing appears in dialogical relationships with Butler's (2015) ideas, from which we intend to draw parallels that enter the field of research from science. For example, she argues that the act of framing is always an interpretive one. It also has a certain intentionality, although the eye that frames it might not realize the possibilities that the framing might produce. Framing goes beyond a certain context, time, history, and social and cultural relationships. It embraces the field of (re)signification, updating, questioning, images and their negatives, and the relationships of meanings that are constituted in *dialogue*—as populated and constitutive relationships of multiple meanings, in history, in the happenings within the context, and in the here and now, but also the future. They are relationships of responsibility and responsiveness—the condition of existence of dialogical relationships: before a question there must be the possibility of an answer—with and for others who carry within themselves that multiplicity of voices.

Thus, *dialogue* has axiological, theoretical and methodological roots. In other words, it encompasses both an ethical position and a way of doing, a practice in approaching and understanding those relationships that produce meanings—with the voices of others, the unfamiliar ones as well as our own. Those voices are understood as ideas, conceptions of the world, that are expressed in dialogical relationships, that have the freedom to move, to act in times and spaces, to participate actively and responsibly in the future, independently, coexisting with other voices, generating diverse senses in a relationship of *responsiveness*. The voices contain in themselves other voices, which dialogue with voices in other time periods. These voices can express themselves in various ways; some are heard more loudly while others are faint. They remain latent, unspoken, like noises pointing to the future and waiting for the right social, historical and cultural times and spaces to be (re)born.

As such,

> We can think about framing, then, as something active, which both rules out and demonstrates, in silence, without any visible sign of the operation. What emerges from those conditions is a viewer who means to be in an immediate (and irrefutable) visual relationship with reality (Butler, 2015, p. 112).

At the same time, Butler (2015) acknowledges the delimiting function of framing, mediated by the political and social norms that place admissible images in the domain of *representativeness* into focus, hiding the image from perception. Although what is excluded is encrypted in the framing itself, in the in-between, in the *limiar*[2] of what is on display and what remains in the shadows. Thus, framing continues to open an unsuspected range of interpretations, both from what is obvious from the direct relationships with which it is framed, as well as from the visible (in)visibilities of its *porosities*[3] (García, 2018).

Framings *About* Youth

Carrying out studies *about* youth was not the initial intention we were pursuing when we created a research group driven by the need to scrutinize and understand what our teaching practices were showing us. Our discomfort as inexperienced university professors, in a new context, not only for ourselves but also for everyone who was involved, became an invaluable opportunity. The universalization of higher education throughout Cuba thus became a rich context of opportunities, capable of becoming new and unprecedented event constellations (Benjamin, 1987).

The universalization of higher education constituted a new socio-educational situation for those who entered this type of study with the intention of becoming university professionals. Those who gained access were mainly people who had been excluded for different reasons from the "traditional ways" of training professionals. What did they find? A curriculum that allowed for increased flexibility; seminar classes as the main way of organizing the student–teacher relationship; and a mentoring relationship as the guiding thread of their evolution (Cordovés, 2010; García, 2010).

These elements created conditions that diminished the rigidity of teaching resources as a guarantee to learning, granting another value to uncertainty, the incomplete nature of knowledge, the emergence of questions, independence and self-management in the appropriation of knowledge, self-education and, therefore, the dynamism of the subjects involved: students–teachers–tutors (García, 2010). In this way, the need for change slowly presented itself as a daily requirement.

The students found themselves in a new situation in which the search for alternatives to learn was imminent, whether or not they were prepared for it. What were the initial concerns in this context? What caught our attention in the students/youth who attended our classes were their *shortcomings*. We systematized these *deficiencies* in the research we conducted on life projects (Osorio, 2009) and learning (Díaz, 2009) *about* psychology majors at the university. So, we began to order and analyze what they were not able to do. These first framings offered strong arguments for other moments, paths and framings in which we relied on the justification of the *deficiencies* that we had unveiled. These included:

- Scant participation in non-obligatory "extra" activities, suggesting a poor development of interests;
- Limited resources for managing interpersonal relationships, with a tendency toward aggressiveness and competition and scarce support for the development of others;
- Preference to work individually and not ask for help;
- Limitations for group work. In the face of tasks that required group formation, students exhibited the propensity to work individually;
- Poor communicative relationships, manifested in oral and written expression and in listening to the criteria set forth;
- Tendency to reproduce in the resolution of tasks;
- Propensity to blame others for their own failures;
- Difficulties in reproducing knowledge, solving simple professional problems and integrating and applying knowledge acquired in various courses;
- Tendency toward execution in the solution of assignments.

At the same time, in research pursuits that, we believed at the time, were attempting to better understand youth and young adults and why they were not producing the results "university students were expected to achieve," we continued to discover and describe other *deficiencies*. On this matter, in his work on life projects of university students, Osorio (2009) noted that among the main priorities of their life projects, professional training was nowhere to be found. Instead, family, work and recreation topped the list. Consequently, they prioritized family, work and recreation in their temporal organization. Likewise, research participants were not interested in other areas of improvement, such as insertion in scientific student groups or other research groups or participation in professional debate spaces. Nor did they carry out bibliographic reviews that would allow them to expand their professional culture. Osorio identified these issues as well as the insufficient development of study habits as some of the causes why students constantly fail exams or drop out of school.

At the same time, we began to identify *shortcomings* in ourselves as teachers. At first blush, we associated our performance in our roles with fear, since we found ourselves before a situation that we had never experienced before. Our closest relationships clung to the lecturer model, in which a more or less engaged interaction with students is maintained, depending on course design and pedagogy (Cordovés, 2010; García, 2010).

Faced with this situation of uncertainty, we began to wonder if we were somehow acting like *didactist*[4] teachers. Reflections on the behavior of traditionalist teachers by Fariñas and Torre (2001, apud. Fariñas, 2005) allowed us to identify, from this framing, that:

1. We were acting from a position of power from which we attributed to ourselves knowledge of which students were ignorant. This implies a certain sense of security around our performance as teachers based on a relationship in which one gives orders and teaches and the other learns and obeys.
2. We were acting under the assumption that didactic resources guaranteed solid learning of the contents that we were teaching. Thus, we stripped the apprentices of their responsibility in learning and we overestimated our roles as teachers.
3. Consequently, the ways we were lesson planning *for* students tended to supplant their responsibility in the appropriation of knowledge.
4. This also implied the existence of normative demands that provided criteria for desirable behaviors and inhibited the course of creative behaviors that strayed from what was "stipulated." This standardization does not only include problem solving and learning. It also extended into interpersonal relationships. Thus, the meanings of "good student," "good professional" and "good teacher" were established. There was only room for "what must be."
5. We resisted embracing diversity as an expression of what is human, which manifested in prejudices against the massification of the study of psychology and the backgrounds of our students.[5] This constituted a particularly powerful behavior that prompted the stigmatization of individuals and discrimination against them based on sex, age, race, learning skills, physical appearance, life stories, etc.

Thus, we realized that it was necessary to make changes, including to our teaching methods. This required a (de)(re)structuration of points of reference and practices in order to aid in the development of students to empower them to assume self-direction in their own professional formation in these new conditions. It, therefore, became necessary for us to create conditions that would allow for a relationship of dependence–independence in learning dynamics that would stimulate students' responsibility in the acquisition of knowledge oriented to professional problem solving and to impact their lives. With this, we were attempting to contribute to the training of professionals who would efficiently insert themselves into the latticework of relationships inherent in their current social duties.

To promote this development, changes must be oriented to honing in on social problems and temporal organization. They must also meet the need for a complex appreciation of the phenomena under study as seen from different angles; and offer the possibility of involving teachers in this need for change. This new orientation required us to refocus our lenses and achieve other framings, different from the ones we had been using up to that point—fixated on *shortcomings*, the obvious and past–present relationships (García, 2010). It also demanded us to transgress/surpass the boundaries of psychology (Cordovés, 2017).

When we changed our focus, our gaze changed, from an *a priori* framing to one produced by letting ourselves be surprised by contexts and relationships. We consider both research projects planned *a priori* and adventures *with* the field to be sensitive to framings, times and spaces, records of daily activities, delimited by choices made by those who relate to them from different positions. They continue to be "acts of delimitation" that are potentially interpretive (Butler, 2015). Nevertheless, the framings that chose us in the field of research embrace a multitude of new meanings, open to each update and verification, and undoubtedly offer other possibilities for research in the humanities and social sciences. These meanings are far from "representing" and "proving" social, cultural and individual events (García, 2018).

Likewise, those first framings based on *deficiencies* left out all the richness hidden behind them and led us down traditional paths in our practices of teaching and research. Thus, we were surprised to find ourselves reproducing the same ways of doing and researching, studying reality as if it were a photograph—static—and, in so doing, hiding its movements that take place in the domains of the in-between, the *limiar*, the shadows. This happens because in the face of new scenarios that demand new forms of practices, empowerment and skills, we tended to act based on references to the prevailing ways of doing (Cordovés, 2010,

2017; García, 2010; Marsico, 2012). In any case, these are movements we need to make transparent because they express porous relationships, "insignificant details" and minutiae that constitute and at the same time are constituted by the (in)tense dialogues that take place in those temporal-spatial confluences (García, 2018).

However, opening ourselves up to adventures and letting ourselves be surprised are attitudes, stances toward research that should set the courses of researchers in the so-called "social sciences." There is nothing predetermined in this field, nothing that keeps directions fixed, nothing with a beginning and an end, a first and last word. All people and things have porous existences in the *limiar*. They have voices and silences waiting to be (re)born. Everything takes place in a sort of unfolded existence, to paraphrase Vigotsky (2001), in a *limiar*, in conditions of porous relationships that—as they are uncovered, auscultated and shared—help to learn to (un)know the events we study. This is a stance that we intend to adopt on our paths, but not without first acknowledging that it is difficult and not always successful.

Many times, we walk down one-way streets driven by the need, sometimes personal and sometimes imposed, to follow them under the assumption that they are free from stones and obstacles, or with the plan to decipher them and their possibilities. However, this is not the "reality" of the research process. It has two-way streets, alleys, shortcuts and unsuspected paths that we must follow, listen to, smell, walk and (re)signify as we travel them.

This challenge, which is that of the *participative mindset*, of being open to the experiences of other people and things, of letting ourselves be surprised, of examining reality beyond the obvious and being interested in the minutiae and the "in-between." It is there, according to Zanella (2017), where a variety of possibilities always exists; openings, detours, queries and transgressions. It appears with its own demands and theoretical-methodological implications. One of these is to abandon the stance of doing research *about* and start doing research *with*.

> Only by traveling *with* the city, *with* people, *with* the field, *with* others' experiences, in *dialogues*, is knowledge (re)created. Other meanings emerge, fissures to other possibilities are created, and the research and researchers are prompted to queries, estrangements, the need to auscultate, in the vestiges of times, the echoes of the voices that populated each space; the need to reveal the (in)visibles that were left behind a planned and

guided path aimed at a certain objective. It is in these relationships that the power to venture in unsuspected directions emerges (García, 2018, p. 49).

This is the way that doing research *with* demands us to distance ourselves from the vices of linear and dichotomous thinking and experience new ways of thinking, asking and searching. It demands a transition from the limits of the disciplinary to the transdisciplinary, the polyphonic, the porous, heteroglossia as the conditions for more encompassing practices (Cordovés, 2017).

Frames *with* Youth

On our paths of re-positioning our teaching and research practices from new stances, we have been moving our framings in two fundamental directions of analysis, which for moments complement each other, blend and diverge. One of them is committed to the creation of conditions to study development. The other ponders research assuming a historical understanding.

The understanding of development from a historical perspective rests on addressing time through the multiple possibilities that are revealed in its evolution, such that the present contains the multiplicity of past voices and the seeds of the future, highlighting the role of the person in its construction. This evolution allows us to unveil and analyze the relationships of the conditions that blend and dialogue *with* multiple events, in an apparent (dis)(re)organization of time and a detour from the paths, showing the powers of the side streets, alleyways and fissures of times and spaces in the production of knowledge.

In this direction, studies on lifestyles *with* youth under conditions of universalized education stand out (García, 2010). Lifestyle is understood as the unique way in which the times and spaces of life are subjectified in cooperation with other times and spaces of life that share a particular culture and history. This unique way is, according to Fariñas (2005, p. 89), "...a psychological situation created by the subject that bears the imprint of the personality and conditions its development." García's work ponders an analysis based on indicators of lifestyle development. Based on these points of reference, the multiple ways in which youth (re)create strategies in the relationships they establish with their developmental conditions are revealed, based on the histories of relationships that constitute and have already constituted the young participants in the research experience in their own evolution. On this matter, García highlights that:

1. The development parameters that were analyzed *with* youth are expressed in a harmonic, synergistic and coherent relationship. In the latticework of the parameters of system, internality and effectiveness, we see the emergence of the indicators that essentially guide the direction of participants' development, the process of conducting their lives that tentatively defines them. However, when evaluating the parameters of history, refinement and energization, indicators that appear as a personal seal and as resources that allow young people to craft, with greater or lesser quality, their lives are more clearly outlined.
2. The perspective of the theoretical-methodological analysis of lifestyle we employed:

    (a) facilitates the understanding of young people based on the expression of the unique and typical ways in which they conduct their lives. It reveals the unique relationships they establish with the different contexts of development with which they interact and the assessments they make in the evolution of their (self-) development. It serves as an indicator of their involvement in their development, which becomes a tendency that define their life histories.
    (b) benefits the understanding of personality development by offering the possibility of entering the process of configuring complex psychological formations (e.g., worldview, professional motivations, self-worth, life projects) based on (self-)reflective, conscious, (self-)transforming and regulating processes that take place within youth in the process of (re)creating their social and private times and spaces.
    (c) allows us to evaluate youth in relation to contexts, making it possible to assess the ways in which the relations they establish with those contexts stimulate the emergence of development and benefit (or not) the dynamics of (self-)education.

In sum, first, studying lifestyles has an invaluable diagnostic value, as it offers us the possibility of carrying out an analysis of the potential of young people, the resources they possess to relate to educational contexts and the emergence of development. It reveals the movements and dynamics of youth development as evolution in their histories. Second, the appropriation of new resources that prime the process of ingraining a lifestyle of development is not yet an indicator of development in the research participants. Finally, the stories of these youth rely on established personal resources to craft their lives in new developmental contexts.

For his part, Cordovés (2010) set out to create certain conditions of learning-development to accompany the paths of development of young adults in his research. It is an understanding of development based on what Fariñas (2005) calls an ethically positive sense: "the subject's creative involvement in culture and its greatest expression, the formation of personality" (p. 88). This translates into favoring the creative involvement of young people in the professional world through the resolution of learning tasks. For these tasks to constitute learning-development conditions, they should meet the following requirements:

1. To allow the pupil to professionally address a social problem in such a way as to satisfy his/her professional training needs—e.g., learning, passing college courses, sharpening their professional tools, etc.—that also have personal benefits.
2. To be diverse and traverse university disciplines and courses, stimulating the dynamics of "learning to learn."
3. To prioritize in their organization and design learning new content and developing new personal resources (e.g., professional tools) over the solution of a specific problem as such, creating a relationship of participation and exchange between pupil and professor or other professional.
4. To promote an environment (e.g., mentoring relationship) that learners perceive as a space to satisfy their growing needs (e.g., cognitive, creative, stress reduction, communication, recognition) and recognize themselves as a development opportunity for the teacher.
5. To prioritize the development of strategic learning skills that support their professional (self-)formation over traditional forms of student evaluations.

The creation of these tasks is based on an understanding of development in motion, which expresses the dialogical relationships of people with culture(s) and with themselves beyond the obvious and evident. A development that takes place in conditions of activity and communication as complex frameworks of relationships that constitute the social situation of development, and which must be supported by psychological resources of a strategic nature.

Based on his educational intervention that adopted these precepts, Cordovés (2010) recognized that:

- The relationships that young people established with the task they had to solve promoted the emergence of the development of "learning to learn."
- Considering the position that young people assume in the production of their development, pupils took on their professional self-education with greater initiative and action, suggesting the emergence of independence.
- Intentional non-reflection, despite being aware of learning resources, is the most recurrent trend among those who jeopardize the development of independence by youth.

Our work described above was analyzed by Fariñas (2013), who highlighted that the research strategy we followed can lead to:

- achieving an environment of collective work that may motivate self-development and personal–professional improvement;
- assigning of professional tasks to students while taking care of the comprehensive evolution of their personalities;
- clarifying the ways in which certain processes and characteristics emerge in youth, which is a key and distinctive element in the development of each individual;
- demonstrating the value of this way of organizing the analysis of human development, allowing a dynamic vision of what happens through the influence professors exert on students.

Framing (Dis)Adjustments

Placing ourselves in a critical relationship with our own acts, that is, with our research projects, their framings and their movements allows us to perform constant evaluative exercises in which we try to express diverse meanings. Bourdieu (2012) and Tassinari (2012) alerted us to the complexities of analyzing what constitutes us and what we constitute. This requires an exercise in estrangement when it is necessary to de-naturalize our own practices (Zanella, 2017).

Thus, we consider that the works we have discussed in this paper, even with their potentialities and openings, also contain limitations. Framing, which relies almost exclusively on categories that are proposed to us, keeps us in some ways in the (in)visible domains of the disciplines that impose limits on investigative thought and action. Employing this approach at the time of our research projects, allowing for "movements" within, did not reveal all the possibilities that our research offered us for delving into the complexities of development. Nor did it allow us to totally transcend the domain of limits and to venture into the powerful domain of the in-between, the *limiar*.

Framing research from the discipline of psychology, in this case, as the only movement of the lens, even if that lens encompasses positions within it that allow for other experiences in understanding development, is one of the "naturalizations" that must be transcended. This makes it difficult for us to see the complexity of what we are trying to understand and can inhibit all its movements from emerging. If we assume that development occurs in relationships and that it has a socio-historical and cultural character, then it is necessary to understand these relationships from the conditions in which they occur. Consequently, it is necessary to study social, historical and cultural dynamics. In this sense, we cannot understand/produce without the possibility of dialogues, without stopping to listen to the polyphony of times, spaces, development contexts, sociological, anthropological and historical productions, and without listening to other ways of doing, dialoguing and understanding.

Those are the relationships we consider powerful enough to understand the movement and evolution of frames, as with the Bakhtinian notion (2012) that there is no beginning and end point or a first and last word. There is a point of (re)creation in which perhaps something dies, but other possibilities (re)constitute, (re)invent and are constantly (re)born in relations of socio-historical and cultural conditions.

The challenge of conducting research *with* young people not only requires proposing certain learning-development conditions to them. Research should also constitute a possibility for personal–professional growth for those who perform the research. This is a necessary framing given that research *with* would not only be interested in people who, in other perspectives, would be called "research subjects." *With* is not a simple change of words; it is not just a semantic variation. It is not enough to substitute one word for another when what it is about and what nourishes change is an ethical—and dialogic—concern for the relationships with the people with whom the research is done (Zanella, 2017). Those who conduct that research project are also being researched, i.e., they are framed, questioned and subjected to new conditions. Therefore, the participant mindset of opening ourselves up to the experience of others is opening ourselves up to experiencing ourselves as well.

Another one of the potentialities revealed through our research history is the understanding of the researcher's role. To exchange the vertical positions of "power" for positions of reciprocal learning, where hierarchies do not exist, becomes a valuable condition for the relationships *with* who/what we dialogue, in a process of two-way (re)creations, of processes that have several perspectives.

As limitations transformed into potential for new paths and research projects, the meanings generated in our previous dialogues were listening and dialoguing with other voices, renewing and being reborn in other challenges to be addressed in other times and spaces, on new paths that found us and where we found ourselves. Now we continue walking, always with the certainty of having the lens open to attachments, estrangements, thoughts that make us uneasy, possibilities and new framings.

Notes

1. We use this term in the sense of sociocultural conditions, following the work of the Russian psychology Lev Vigotsky (1999, 2001).
2. The point of departure for our use of the concept *limiar* are Vigotsky's (1999) and Gagnebin's (2014) ideas. *Limiar* belongs to the realm of temporary spaces, like relationships in movement and transition, as of yet opened and unfinished. It is not a limit or boundary; it is indetermination, uncertainty, insecurity, disorder, (dis)harmony, journey and evolution. It is a relationship that indicates an analysis in which relationships and dichotomous positions are eliminated

in order to contemplate what is in between, hidden, invisible. It is the polyphonic relationship in which several voices-ideas coexist in (dis)harmony.

3. We adopted Benjamin's (1987) concept of porosity, i.e., the ability some things have to become another, new, without drying up into something fixed and permanent. In this way, our perspective can go beyond dualities, delving into the *limiar* to perceive what lies in between.
4. We adopted Fariñas' ideas (2005, p. 182) to define *didactism* as the exaggeration of didactical processes and control of students' behavior and development. The English translation is an adoption from the Spanish word, *didactista*.
5. This refers to the universalization of higher education that began in Cuba in 2001. Among other objectives, it sought to democratize access to higher education in Cuba. A deeper analysis can be found in Cordovés (2010) and García (2010).

Bibliography

Bakhtin, M. (1999). *Estética de la creación verbal* (10th ed.). Siglo XXI.

Bakhtin, M. (2012 [1924]). *Para uma filosofia do ato responsável* (2nd ed., V. Viotello & C. A. Faraco, Trans.). Pedro & João Editores.

Benjamin, W. (1987). *Rua de mão única. Obras escolhidas II*. Editora Brasiliense.

Bourdieu, P. (2012). *Sur l'État. Cours au Collège de France,1989–1992*. Seuil.

Butler, J. (2015). *Quadros de guerra: quando a vida é passível de luto?* Civilização Brasileira.

Cordovés, A. (2010). *Caracterización de las dinámicas de aprender a aprender en estudiantes de psicología en la Universidad de Holguín* (unpublished master's thesis). Universidad de La Habana, Cuba.

Cordovés, A. (2017). *Caminantes y caminos que se hacen al andar. Trajetórias de professoras/es de ensino médio em Cuba* (unpublished doctoral dissertation). Universidade Federal de Santa Catarina, Brasil.

Díaz, A. (2009). *Aprender a aprender en estudiantes de Psicología: una propuesta de intervención histórico culturalista* (unpublished undergraduate thesis). Universidad de Holguín, Cuba.

Fariñas, G. (2004). *Maestro: para una didáctica del aprender a aprender*. Pueblo y Educación.

Fariñas, G. (2005). *Psicología, educación y sociedad. Un estudio sobre el desarrollo humano*. Félix Varela.

Fariñas, G. (2013). *A propósito de la imaginación (Educación y desarrollo humano)*. Félix Varela.

Gagnebin, J. M. (2014). *Limiar, aura e rememoração. Ensaios sobre Walter Benjamin* (1ª ed.). Editora 34.

García, D. (2010). *Caracterización del estilo de vida en estudiantes de Psicología de la sede universitaria municipal Holguín* (unpublished master's thesis). Universidad de La Habana, Cuba.

García, D. (2018). *Tensões tempo-corpo na Escuela Cubana de Ballet* (unpublished doctoral dissertation). Universidade Federal de Santa Catarina, Brasil.

Marsico, G. (2012). The double uncertainty: Trajectories and professional identityin changing contexts. *Culture and Psychology, 18*(1), 121–132. https://doi.org/10.1177/1354067X11427469

Osorio, C. (2009). *La formación profesional como dirección del proyecto de vida en un grupo de trabajadores sociales que estudian psicología en la sede universitaria municipal Holguín* (unpublished undergraduate thesis). Universidad de Holguín, Cuba.

Tassinari, A. (2012). A Sociedade Contra a Escola. In A. Tassinari, B. Grando & M. Albuquerque (Eds.), *Educação Indígena: reflexões sobre noções nativas de infância, aprendizagem e escolarização* (Vol. 1, pp. 275–294). Universidade Federal de Santa Catarina.

Vigotsky, L. (1999). *A tragédia de Hamlet, Príncipe de Dinamarca*. Martins Fontes.

Vigotsky, L. (2001). *Psicologia da arte* (2ª ed.). Martin Fontes.

Zanella, A. (2017). *Entre galerias e museus: diálogos metodológicos no encontro da arte com a ciência e a vida*. Pedro & João Editores.

CHAPTER 6

Intersections Between Temporal Organization and Life Projects Among Young Adults

Carlos Manuel Osorio García, Richard N. Gioioso, Zaily Leticia Velázquez Martínez, and Miguel E. Bringuez Chacón

Introduction

Soon after the triumph of the Cuban revolution, specifically in 1961, the new government began to devote special attention and effort to the eradication of poverty and the increase in the level of cultural awareness and knowledge among the population. Cuban leader Fidel Castro Ruz commented on this topic, saying: "We must fight a war against the

This chapter was translated by Yoenia Iñiguez Ricardo.

C. M. O. García · Z. L. V. Martínez · M. E. B. Chacón
Universidad de Holguín, Holguín, Cuba
e-mail: cmosorio@uho.edu.cu

Z. L. V. Martínez
e-mail: zaily@uho.edu.cu

R. N. Gioioso et al. (eds.), *Youth and Development in Cuba*,
https://doi.org/10.1007/978-3-030-90866-9_6

dearth of culture. How? By training music, theater and dance instructors" (Velázquez, 2005, p. 3). The country's leadership thus set out to the task of creating specialized schools to train art instructors, known in Spanish as *escuelas de instructores de arte*, in which roughly 6,000 professionals were educated and subsequently worked for more than 40 years to bring cultural awareness and education to the Cuban population beginning in primary school. During the 1990s, the training of art instructors was limited due to the so-called Special Period, i.e., the desperate economic conditions in the country caused by the fall of the Soviet bloc. By the year 2000, however, the Cuban government revitalized programs aimed at benefiting children, teenagers and young adults in several fields such as education, culture, social development and health. Part of this movement was the founding of new *escuelas de instructores de arte*, renewing the objective of bringing culture to all corners of the island and placing Cuba among the countries with the highest levels of academic achievement among its inhabitants in the world (Velázquez, 2005).

The creation of a corps of art instructors offered Cuban young adults the opportunity to enter a specialized position within the field of education and a new source of employment for them. Young adults who take up the work of art instructors pursue the development and dissemination of artistic-cultural knowledge and appreciation to the infant-youth population, primarily through workshops in educational facilities. In this sense, the work of these young adult professionals makes it possible to transform the sociocultural scenario and to promote a lifestyle among the Cuban population that integrates artistic, human and patriotic dimensions to foster the assimilation of critical judgment and aesthetic preferences from an early age (Velázquez, 2005).

Taking into account the historical relevance of culture in society and in the Cuban educational landscape since the early 1960s, and by extension the relevance of the workforce composed primarily of young adults, we decided to target this group of art instructors for a research project.

M. E. B. Chacón
e-mail: mebringuez@nauta.cu

R. N. Gioioso (✉)
Saint Joseph's University, Philadelphia, USA
e-mail: rgioioso@sju.edu

In the past ten years, there has been a small proliferation of research on Cuban youth and young adults, especially in the field of psychology, focused on their *temporal organization* in various developmental contexts, such as self-employment, teaching, tourism and university settings.[1] We carried out our research in the city of Holguín, capital of the province of Holguín, the largest of its 14 municipalities and the third biggest city in Cuba (ONEI, 2017). The city of Holguín has the largest group of instructors in the province and offers cultural education to students in three different artistic genres—music, theater and dance. These characteristics make it an ideal setting to study arts instructors in an urban setting.

In several previous informal visits to our research sites in Holguín, we recorded some interesting observations that motivated the development of our formal research project. For instance, we discovered that administratively speaking art instructors receive oversight and direction from both the Ministry of Education and the Ministry of Culture, which requires them to duplicate their adherence to guidelines and criteria, resulting in the need to respond to two sets of demands. This added layer of burden and distraction appeared to detract from the time available to them to plan cultural activities in school. One young adult art instructor expressed her dissatisfaction with this aspect of her job, emphasizing that the creative process can be slow and requires both time and focus. Furthermore, the quantity and intensity of the demands from both Ministries constrain their time and therefore productivity, causing them to complete their tasks late, despite their efforts to be responsible and engaged with their assignments. We also observed their tendencies to postpone important tasks and activities without setting concrete deadlines in the future.

Due to these observations and the decisive role that temporal organization plays in the successful development of individuals in different areas and contexts of daily life, in the creative act and in the effective execution of life projects, we decided to examine the characteristics of *temporal organization* that drive the *life projects* of young adult art instructors that work at a primary schools in the municipality of Holguín.

Concretely, we sought to answer the following questions:

- What are the main life projects of these young adult art instructors?
- To what spheres of daily life do they devote their time?
- Have they managed to develop the skills of temporal organization?

  - Which skills do they have and to what extent are they developed?
- Is temporal organization a means for them to achieve their life projects?

Based on previous research, we formulated the following hypothesis: Young adult art instructors who work in elementary schools in Holguín will not have developed temporal organization skills in their daily life, which limit the successful achievement of their life projects in the medium- and long-terms. In the balance of this chapter, we present a brief discussion of the theoretical background used in the study of life projects and temporal organization, as well as the methodological approaches that made our inquiry possible. We then present and analyze the results of our study, followed by conclusionary remarks on our findings and future considerations for the study of young adults, temporal organization and life projects.

Life Projects, Temporal Organization and Human Development in Youth and Young Adulthood

During youth and young adulthood, individuals assume different responsibilities, roles and functions in the diverse spheres of daily life according to their interests, values, motivations and needs. Those elements mark the development of objectives, goals, actions and activities that mediate the fulfillment of life projects.[2] In this chapter, we follow Dominguez and Ibarra's (2003, p. 448) conceptualization of *future projection*, defined as:

> ...the structuration and integration of a set of reasonings refined in a future temporal perspective, for the medium or the long term, which has an elevated emotional meaning or personal importance to the subject and of the corresponding strategies for the achievement of the objectives set.

Thus, in our analysis of *life projects* we assumed four commonly used dimensions employed for analyses of this nature since the 1990s.[3] These dimensions and their empirical indicators are the basis upon which we collected and analyzed our data, examining their relevance, feasibility and level of material realization by our research participants. The four dimensions are: *content*, *strategies*, *temporality* and *obstacle prediction*.

Content refers to the spheres of the system of activities and communication to which the life project is oriented. These include: schooling and study, work-profession, family of origin, created family, partner, interpersonal relationships, recreation, traveling, material needs, among others. *Strategies* are composed of the means and actions by which the subject intends to achieve the life projects s/he has defined; these are classified as structured, partially structured, not-structured or not defined. *Temporality* refers to the time frame in which the achievement of the life project is located; time frames can be short-, medium-, long- or undefined term. The last dimension, *obstacle prediction*, considers the aptitude of the subject to identify contingencies that may affect the realization of his/her projects; the contingencies are differentiated as external factors, internal factors and mixed.

As you can see, *temporality* is one of the four fundamental dimensions of life projection and the creation and execution of life projects. However, it is important to note that the achievement of life projects does not only depend on defining temporal periods, e.g., short- or long-term. Instead, success also requires the development of other abilities, specifically *temporal organization*.

Empirical studies on temporal organization started in 1954, when the term was first introduced (Claessens et al., 2007), and from then on, scholars have tended to define it as a competence, capacity or ability.[4] In this chapter we use the term and concept of *temporal organization of daily life*, understood as a general ability that forms human development. From the Cultural-Historical approach, which emanated from Séve's (1975) theory of activity, it is specifically understood as an infrastructure of personality. We follow Fariñas' (2004, p. 55) employment of the concept as "personality dynamics (attitudes, values, actions, feelings, etc.) that enable us to perform intentional temporal projection, especially in the present–future, with the objective of better self-governing our lives." The structure of the ability of temporal organization includes four actions (pp. 100–102):

- *Planning of meaning* orients the motivational hierarchies of the individual. These hierarchies can be established for different terms (short, medium, long).
- *Control of conditions* refers to analyses an individual performs of the situations in which his/her activities take place regularly, from both

a subjective and an objective point of view. It allows for a more appropriate and realistic organization of life.

- *Probable prediction* delimits time intervals and quantities of time (e.g., one year, 50 minutes) in which activities, relationships and life tasks are estimated to take place. It reflects "flexible anticipation," the ability to adapt to changing circumstances and factors that require actions, e.g., to cancel, to postpone, to extend.
- *Control of results* is a thoughtful assessment of what s/he has done with some degree of frequency and level of awareness.

The actions that make up the structure of the ability to temporally organize help us characterize and determine its level of development. For this, we must take into account a set of indicators that reflect the development of this ability. These include alternating activities with diverse objectives (e.g., among productive, intimate-personal communication, rest, recreation); intentionally planning life routines; breaking life routines; decreasing the number of unfinished tasks and stress; accepting and adapting to eventualities; adequately discerning between importance and the urgency of a task; feeling a sense of satisfaction and the happiness that accompanies it; among others that may emerge from data analysis.[5]

Methodology and Analysis: Configurations of Life Projects and Temporal Organization Among Young Adult Art Instructors in Holguín

The data used in this chapter were collected by researchers from two different nuclei: (1) the Center of Psychosocial Orientation for Human Development in the Department of Psychology at the University of Holguín, from 2015 to 2017; and (2) the student research group "Human Development in Educational Contexts" during the same time period.[6] The methodology employed to gather and analyze the data was qualitative in nature. Principal investigators recruited the young adult art instructors as research participants, four in total.[7] Of them, three were women and one man. Two of them specialized in music, one in theater, and the other in dance. Their ages range from 24 to 28, and each has worked as an art instructor for between 6 and 10 years.

Martha is 28 years old, has completed her university studies, specializing in dance for the past 10 years. *Sandra*, 24 years old, has completed her university studies and has worked as a music instructor for the past 6 years. *Pedro* is 27 years old and has been a theater instructor for 9 years. Finally, Rocío, 24 years old, has worked as a music instructor for the past 6 years. Neither Pedro nor Rocío has finished their university degrees yet.

In our process of inquiry, we used several data collection instruments. For instance, the *pie graph* technique "consists of asking the subject to subdivide a circle in parts, just like a pie, but the parts do not have to be equal, they will represent the amount of time subjects devote to the main activities they develop in their lives" (Suárez, 2007, p. 36). It allows us to know to which activities the individual devotes his/her time and to what extent s/he performs them systematically. We implemented a *structured interview* tool to capture data on how participants temporally organize their lives. Finally, we asked our research subjects to write two *compositions* to describe in their own words: "How I organize my time" to characterize their temporal organization; and "My life project" to determine participants' main life projects.

Life Projects Among Young Adult Art Instructors

To examine and analyze the life projects of the young adult art instructors who participated in our study, we employ the dimensions discussed above: *content*, *strategies*, *temporality* and *obstacle prediction*.

Exploring the *content* of life projects allows us to understand the aspirations, goals and objectives of the four participants, who generally converge regarding how they see themselves in the future. Among all four there is an evident concern or need regarding their professional growth. In the case of Rocío and Pedro, this professional growth is related to the culmination of their university studies. Rocío is currently enrolled and Pedro intends to "go back to the university and get a degree" in the next semester.[8] However, in the case of Martha and Sandra, who already have completed their university degrees, neither has set a new goal of postgraduate education. Rather, they associate furthering their professional growth within their workplace specifically; that is, related to their current economic needs, which can be satisfied better by working than studying. As such, these perceptions regulate their behavior. For Pedro and Sandra, their jobs as art instructors help to satisfy their economic needs, while they have also integrated as members of professional groups of theater and music, respectively.

Martha articulates her desire "to be a better professional, more optimistic, more determined," however, we were not able to identify clear actions that demonstrate objective planning to attain her stated goal. Instead, she appears to conform with social expectations and norms rooted in chauvinism, in which women dedicate themselves to the care of their husbands, children and household chores as her current priorities. For Martha, work is just a source of income. We observed a sense of professional stagnation in her, exemplified by her self-observations that she should be "more determined and stronger in all senses of the word."

Our participants' desires to emigrate from Holguín to Havana, the capital, or out of the country, either temporarily or indefinitely, stand out and merit examination. Specifically, Sandra and Rocío hope to find jobs and personal fulfillment outside of Cuba. Sandra "would like to play [music] on a cruise ship through Europe," "travel to different countries and live in Italy," while Rocío wants to leave Cuba and live in the United States. There, she wants to "find a good job" and be with her family and her father; in her own words, this is her "dream," which drives her to perform certain tasks, like learning English. Martha's desire is to join her family in Havana. She is curious to see places outside of Cuba, but she does not express any desire to live permanently in another country. She would like "to travel to any country in the world one day, not to live there, but to get to know other places." Both Rocío and Martha exhibit signs of the need for affection and filiation, which drives their plans to move away from their current developmental context, i.e., Holguín. Finally, Pedro desires "to travel abroad in the future and help my mother and sister." Rocío, Pedro and Sandra see the best opportunity for professional growth and economic improvement in leaving Cuba, while Martha believes she can achieve that in Havana. In one way or another, it is evident that Holguín is not the place where these young adult art instructors think they can achieve their goals. Despite being a city with a lively cultural-artistic movement, there are limitations to opportunities for economic improvement and employment options.

Family reunification is a decisive driver of both internal and external migration in Cuba, and it figures prominently among our research participants' life projects. Martha wants "to move to Havana to be closer to my mother and stepfather." Sandra wants to "live with her husband in [Italy] and have two children, a boy and a girl." Rocío wants "to be [in the United States] with my father who is alone…so that we can all be together and that our son can have his parents and grandfather close." Some characteristic aspects of the Cuban developmental context and identity stand out in the above examples, including the affective connection with their parents for Martha and Rocío. This is an element that is rooted in the inculcation of family values and constant support both economically and emotionally that is typical in Cuban families. Among our research participants, data show a strong connection with family of origin continues even after they have established a family of their own. For Pedro and Sandra, who are not yet parents, there is an apparent desire to form a family of their own and have children, a concrete life project for the future.

Concern over meeting material needs and expanding material security and comfort is another life project common to all four participants. Sandra says that she wants to go to Italy "to help my family in everything I can, to help my friends...to have everything I need." Pedro wants "to be able to sleep on a good mattress, eat good food, and have a car, at least an old one." Rocío wants "to find a good job in the United States so that my family can live well and have everything we need." And finally, Martha maintains the idea of "moving to Havana...to have better conditions in my home and give my daughter a better future."

It is worth reiterating that emigration is the key element necessary to achieve other life projects, like the formation of their own families with children for Pedro and Sandra, or family reunification for Martha and Rocío. To improve their current economic situation and to find better jobs, these young adults visualize themselves in a context outside of the city and province of Holguín, to Havana for Martha, and in another country for Rocío, Pedro and Sandra.

We now turn to *strategies*, the second dimension of life projects, which refer to the concrete plans, steps and actions currently taking place and that will take place in the future to achieve defined projects. We classify the data gathered from our research participants to evaluate the quality of their planning process into three categories: structured, partially structured or non-structured. Rocío is the only research participant with a *structured strategy* vis-à-vis her intentions to increase her professional preparation. To achieve that goal, she is enrolled in university, majoring in Sociocultural Studies, and devotes at least one hour every day to attending class, studying or doing homework assignments.

Partially structured strategies were common and are exemplified by all our research participants. Although they clearly understand what they must do to make their life projects a reality, these young adults are not planning and executing the necessary actions. For example, Martha desires to reunite with her mother and stepfather and give her daughter tangible opportunities for a better future. She has identified the way to do this: migrating to Havana. However, she is taking no action currently to prepare for or facilitate a move to the capital city. Sandra desires to leave Cuba and live in another country to work and earn money to help her family and friends in Holguín, help her aunt and cousin leave the country and play on a cruise ship that travels through Europe. Like Martha, Sandra has not operationalized the necessary actions to attain this project. Rocío desires to be reunified with her father and find a good job to improve her standard of living. To do this, she wants to leave the country. At the moment however, none of her daily activities or time are dedicated to carrying out concrete actions to achieve her goal.

Regarding *temporality*, i.e., the time frame in which an individual expects to achieve his/her life project, our indicators were: short-, medium-, long- and undefined term. Rocío and Pedro equate the time frame to attain the desired level of professional improvement to their completing their university degrees. Rocío demonstrates a longer-term vision, around two years, to finish her degree, which is a life project that pertains to professional development at this stage of her life. Pedro articulates one of his current life projects as returning to his university studies (as opposed to finishing his degree), which reflects a medium-term vision, as he will enroll in the next few months. In contrast, Martha's desire to emigrate from Holguín to Havana and the ideas of Rocío, Pedro and Sandra to leave the country lack any temporal reference whatsoever, i.e., there is no time frame envisioned or set at all.

It is evident from the data that the fulfillment of one life project frequently depends on the attainment of others. Multiple temporalities are, therefore, a part of life projection and require a more advanced level of skill to navigate. Furthermore, the multiple temporalities must align with a pre-established hierarchy and sequence of the contents of multiple life projects and multiple clearly articulated strategies to achieve each project in its own temporality. For example, the life projects of improving their current quality of life, transforming the material conditions of their homes or expanding future opportunities for family members are linked to emigrating out of Holguín by our research participants. Evidence strongly suggests that specifying multiple temporalities proves elusive for the young adult art instructors in our study, as they demonstrate the tendency to leave time frames undefined for life projects that require sequencing.

Finally, regarding *obstacle prediction*, i.e., contingency planning for hurdles that might arise in the process of attaining life projects, we use the categories of internal, external and mixed to describe the hurdles. Data are scarce for this dimension, as none of our research participants employed it in the structuration of their life projects. For example, Martha expressed no objective and concrete appraisal of what obstacles might lie ahead. Furthermore, she seems to evince a certain aloofness or listlessness regarding her life projects: "Life is full of surprises, today we are here, but tomorrow, who knows?" Without any data on obstacle prediction, we are left unable to assess the quality of it. An overall evaluation of Martha's interview data, however, reveals a level of skepticism and uncertainty around the possibility of achieving her life projects. Similarly, Sandra and Pedro express attitudes of doubt that change is possible, and thus they refrain from engaging in temporal organization, strategic planning or contingency planning. The lack of attention to and preparation for future obstacles indicates a deficiency in the structuration of life projects and portends difficulties in their attainment in the future.

To conclude this section, we reiterate the main points discussed above. First, the *content* of the life projects of our research participants are related to professional growth, emigration, family creation or reunification and the improvement of the material conditions of life. Second, the *strategies* used for the fulfillment of those projects are mostly partially structured, which reveal some level of desire and vision, but lack the concrete steps for translating ideas into manifest reality. Third, *temporality* proves to be a significant limitation for the attainment of life projects for two main reasons. First, our research participants generally do not set time frames for their projects. Second, achieving one life project often depends on the prior achievement of another life project that proceeds it in sequence and relies on a different time frame, which is also left undefined. Finally, there is little to no *obstacle prediction*, suggesting little or no interest in or ability to forecast or execute contingency planning. Along with the findings on strategies and temporality above, the absence of obstacle prediction reveals the incomplete structuration of life projects by our young adult art instructors in Holguín.

Temporal Organization of Life Among Young Art Instructors in Holguín

In this section, we analyze the four actions that together form the structure of the ability of temporal organization: *planning of meaning, control of conditions, probability prediction and control of results.*

To begin, we can identify a taxonomy of activities to which Cuban young adults devote their time:

1. time with created family, e.g., spouses, children;
2. work;
3. household chores, e.g., cooking, laundry;
4. time with family of origin;
5. recreation and leisure, e.g., parties, sports, television;
6. educational activities, e.g., studying, class time;
7. professional growth opportunities, e.g., master class, workshop, retreat;
8. personal growth, e.g., meditation, prayer;
9. relationship with significant other, e.g., date night;
10. self-care, e.g., manicure/pedicure, hair salon or barber shop, massage.

These categories aid us in analyzing participants' *planning of meaning*, i.e., the hierarchy of important and urgent activities established by the individual, which determines the time frame and amount of time devoted to their execution. All research participants identified work as their primary activity, to which they devote the most time, making it possible for them to meet their economic and professional needs. In addition to their jobs as art instructors in their elementary schools, Sandra and Pedro also have part-time jobs in their artistic fields, music and theater gigs, respectively. Martha, Sandra and Rocío spend the second most amount of time with their created families, which they identify as a sphere of high affective value and responsibility. Martha and Rocío spend this time taking care of their children and husbands; Sandra dedicates this time to her partner. Household chores and recreation and leisure are the other activities to which these four young adults devote part of their day. For Pedro, spending time with his family of origin occupies second place in his planning of meaning, while Martha, Sandra and Rocío dedicate less time to their parents and siblings. Finally, only Martha and Sandra spend any time on a given day to self-care activities.

From the planning of meaning we can identify temporal organization in the daily lives of our participants. It is oriented first and foremost to work, followed by time spent with created families and families of origin, household chores and recreation and leisure. As the activities to which they devote the most amount of time, they also constitute the most important activities to plan. Furthermore, the *pie graph* and *composition* tools we employed to gather data give a detailed explanation of their daily activities, providing evidence of well-established habits and daily routines, with a tendency to reproduce learned patterns.

For example, Martha describes her daily routine. "I organize my time as follows: during the week, from Monday to Friday, very early in the morning, I tend to my daughter, take her to daycare and help my husband before he goes to work. Then I go to work all day. After work, I come home in the afternoon and I do my chores..." The first thing Sandra does every day when she wakes up is thank God for the new day and for her health. Then she gets ready for work—brushes her teeth, does her hair and gets dressed—and off she goes to work for the rest of the day. For Rocío, "a normal day starts at 6:15 AM when I wake up and prepare breakfast...Later, when I get home from work, I let my son watch TV while I prepare dinner."

Control of conditions is the component of the structure of temporal organization that consists of a consideration of the objective and subjective conditions that influence the feasibility to·execute desired activities. In our research, we perceived very little time or effort spent on assessing the factors or circumstances that could disrupt or aid in the successful completion of daily activities. All of the research participants discussed very specific tasks, more akin to minutiae than evaluating viability and challenges. Martha describes her household chores on Saturdays. Sandra follows a routine for bathing and getting dressed. Pedro spends 50 minutes, from 3:40 PM to 4:30 PM, memorizing his lines for a play. The extent to which the art instructors exercise the skill of conditions control appears to cover *short-term, objective conditions in an automatic and monotonous way*. Nevertheless, Martha appears to take into account some subjective conditions, concretely her own emotional and psychological state of mind, asserting that she needs "to be more optimistic, more determined and stronger in all senses of the word."

As for *probability prediction*, i.e., the flexible and anticipated planning of the activities performed in intervals of days, weeks, months and years or in other time units like minutes or hours, all of the research participants planned their work and family activities *in the short-term*. Pedro demonstrated the ability to plan in the medium-term with his future life project to go back to university and get a degree in Sociocultural Studies, enrolling in classes within the next two months. Data reveal that research participants refrain from using any concrete instruments, e.g., an agenda or appointment book, to concretize their planning on paper or digitally (e.g., using their mobile phones). Without the use of these tools, it is difficult to plan ahead in any time frame because of the likelihood to forget specific appointments or deadlines as well as to jumble them while planning, e.g., double-booking. These tendencies reveal underlying attitudes that are permissive of unexpected changes. Thus, we can detect a level of flexibility, but it lends itself to the unsuccessful execution of actions that are necessary to achieve life projects. Martha, for example, does not see the value in using an agenda because she has "a very good memory." Sandra also deems herself capable of planning without any helpful instruments: "I rely on my own head." Finally, Rocío reveals an even more lax approach to planning; she does things "as they arise in my life."

Regarding the *control of results*, i.e., the periodical and thoughtful assessment of actions and achievements or failures, none of our research participants demonstrated the tendency or interest in performing explicit and constructive *appraisals* of their activities. However, they do show a tendency to *review* their activities daily, usually with a significant other. If her husband gets home in time, Martha chats with him about what they have done during the day. Sandra proves somewhat more intentional regarding conversing with her partner. "I wait for him to get home after work to chat about our days." Similarly, Rocío and her husband work together to clean up the kitchen after dinner, put their son to bed, and then they have "time to talk a little." Although there is a periodicity to these art instructors' conversations about their activities, an intentional and critical assessment is lacking, impeding the development of a more effective temporal organization of daily life.

Conclusion

In this chapter, we have aimed to characterize the level and quality of temporal organization in a group of young adult art instructors in Holguín and how it relates to the completion of their life projects. To close, we offer the following answers to the research questions we posed in the introduction to the chapter.

1. The four young adult art instructors that participated in our research project devote most of their time to work, created family and family of origin, household chores and recreation and leisure.
2. Overall, these young adults do not demonstrate the ability of temporal organization. They prove most developed in the planning of meaning, and least developed in the control of conditions.
3. The main contents of their life projects revolve around professional growth, internal or external emigration, family creation or reunification and meeting material needs.
4. We consider that the effective and efficient attainment of their life projects will be hindered if the limitations in their abilities of temporal organization continue to exist. This is especially the case for life projects that are projected in the medium- and long-term.

Our research with young adults in Holguín has allowed us to identify some commonalities among them, as well as some particularities, to show the diverse ways in which they perform temporal organization in their daily lives to achieve their life projects. This is just one way to evaluate the process of learning and levels of human development among young adults. Ultimately, we seek to contribute to the field of youth and young adult studies to gain a greater understanding of young adults' attitudes and behaviors in order to aid in their attainment of personal satisfaction in life and rich participation in society.

Notes

1. Temporal organization is an ability that creates an infrastructure for the development of personality and lays the foundation to accomplish life projects. See also the following references: Osorio et al. (2017) and Gioioso et al. (2018) on self-employed young adults; Velázquez et al. (2018) on teachers; Tapia (2018) on workers in the tourism industry; and Osorio and Velázquez (2018) and Osorio (2012) about university students.
2. Different terms are used to conceptualize future projection, among which we can find: objectives, goals, ideals and projects. Those

scholars who use a Marxist foundation are particularly relevant to Cuba due to its socioeconomic and political system. See Domínguez and Ibarra (2003) and Domínguez (2003).
3. Domínguez (1997) established these dimensions. See also Pujol and Domínguez (2018) and Oquendo and Domínguez (2018).
4. See also Durán (2012), De Jongh (2012), Trueman and Hartley (1996), Fariñas (2004, 2005, 2008).
5. See also Fariñas (2019).
6. This group was created in 2005 by Alexander A Cordovés PhD and Deysi Emilia García PhD according to A. Cordovés (personal communique, August 24, 2018). More recently, this group was led by Carlos M. Osorio García and Zaily L. Velázquez Martínez, two of the authors of this article. Both professionals and students of psychology and other social sciences compose its membership. Among the objectives of this groups are: to carry out research oriented toward favoring human development in educative contexts; promoting innovative educative practices; favoring scientific debates about human development; among others.
7. We use pseudonyms in this article to protect the identities of our research participants.
8. All data was gathered in Spanish. This and all other quotes from research participants are translations by Gioioso.

Bibliography

Claessens, B., Van Eerde, W., Rutte, C., & Roe, R. (2007). A review of time management literature. *Personnel Review, 36*(2), 255–276. https://doi.org/10.1108/00483480710726136

Domínguez, L. (Ed.). (2003). *Psicología del desarrollo: Adolescencia y juventud. Selección de lecturas*. Editorial Universitaria Félix Varela.

Domínguez, L., & Ibarra, L. (2003). Juventud y proyectos de vida. In L. Domínguez (Ed.), *Psicología del desarrollo: adolescencia y juventud. Selección de lecturas*. Editorial Universitaria Félix Varela.

Domínguez, M. (1997). La juventud en el contexto de la estructura social cubana. Datos y reflexiones. *Papers. Revista De Sociología, 52*, 67–81. https://doi.org/10.5565/rev/papers.1881

Durán, E. (2012). Competencia manejo del tiempo en la formación de profesionales de la administración. *Revista Venezolana De Gerencia, 17*(58), 291–306.

De Jongh, O. (2012). *Perfil de competencias para estudiantes de Psicología* (unpublished undergraduate thesis). Universidad de La Habana, Cuba.

Fariñas, G. (2004). *Maestro, para una didáctica del aprender a aprender.* Editorial Pueblo y Educación.

Fariñas, G. (2005). *Psicología, educación y sociedad. Un estudio sobre el desarrollo humano.* Editorial Universitaria Félix Varela.

Fariñas, G. (2008). *Aprender a aprender en la educación superior: experiencia cubana desde una perspectiva vygotskiana* (pre-conference workshop). Congreso Internacional Universidad 2008 (1–45), La Habana, Cuba.

Fariñas, G. (2019). *Aprendizaje y desarrollo humano desde la teoría de la complejidad. La teoría en la práctica.* Editorial Universitaria Félix Varela.

Gioioso, R., Osorio, C. M., & Velázquez, Z. L. (2018). La organización del tiempo y el cuentapropismo: Un estudio preliminar de jóvenes emprendedores en Holguín, Cuba. *The Latin Americanist, 62*(4), 478–496. https://doi.org/10.1111/tla.12211

ONEI: Oficina Nacional de Estadística e Información. (2017). Access http://www.onei.gob.cu

Oquendo, D., & Domínguez, L. (2018). *Proyectos futuros en mujeres jóvenes embarazadas portadoras y no del VIH-SIDA* (conference presentation). Congreso Internacional de Investigadores sobre Juventud, La Habana, Cuba.

Osorio, C. (2012). *Proyecto de vida en estudiantes de Psicología.* In Memorias de la Jornada Científica de Psicología Aplicada (PSICAP 2012). ISBN: 978-959-16-1457-5.

Osorio, C., Velázquez, Z., & Rodríguez, T. (2017). *La organización del tiempo en jóvenes cuentapropistas. Reflexiones para un análisis desde la perspectiva de género* (conference presentation). II Convención Internacional de Ciencias Sociales y Ambientales, Santiago de Cuba. ISBN: 978-959-207-577-1.

Osorio, C., & Velázquez, Z. (2018). *Estudio de las habilidades de organización temporal en estudiantes de Psicología* (conference presentation). VIII Convención en Psicología (HOMINIS 2018), La Habana, Cuba. ISBN: 978-959-16-4154-0.

Pujol, C., & Domínguez, L (2018). *Proyectos futuros de jóvenes con cardiopatías congénitas corregidas* (conference presentation). Congreso Internacional de Investigadores sobre Juventud, La Habana, Cuba.

Séve, L. (1975). *Marxismo y teoría de la personalidad.* Amorrortu Editores.

Suárez, L. (2007). *Un acercamiento al desempeño profesional de los maestros de la enseñanza primaria* (unpublished undergraduate thesis). Universidad de La Habana, Cuba.

Tapia, C. (2018). *Estudio sobre la organización temporal en jóvenes trabajadores del turismo que presentan síntomas de estrés* (unpublished undergraduate thesis). Universidad de Holguín, Cuba.

Trueman, M., & Hartley, J. (1996). A comparison between the time-management skills and academic performance of mature and traditional-entry university students. *Higher Education, 32*(2), 199–215. https://doi.org/10.1007/BF00138396

Velázquez, M. (2005). *Formación de instructores de arte. La experiencia cubana* (pre-conference workshop). Congreso Internacional de Pedagogía, La Habana, Cuba.

Velázquez, Z., Osorio, C., & Peña, Y. (2018). *La organización del tiempo en maestros jóvenes* (conference presentation). Congreso de Investigadores sobre Juventud, La Habana, Cuba.

CHAPTER 7

Journalism Students' Conceptions of Gender Violence Against Women in Relationships

Aida T. Torralbas Fernández and Sandra Fagales Mir

Opening the Analysis

Journalism could be a profession comparable only to teaching in terms of social influence. Through mass media, journalists can build realities and legitimize social imaginaries, thus gaining a powerful space that becomes strategic and has to be taken into account when projecting the desired models of society. The journalistic treatment that is made of any topic of social content could be, for the population that receives it, either a

This chapter was translated by Doralkis Ramírez Ronda.

A. T. Torralbas Fernández (✉)
Psychology Department, Universidad Central de Las Villas, Universidad de Holguín, Holguín, Cuba

S. Fagales Mir
Department of Institutional Communication, Universidad de Holguín, Holguín, Cuba
e-mail: amelip@nauta.cu

R. N. Gioioso et al. (eds.), *Youth and Development in Cuba*,
https://doi.org/10.1007/978-3-030-90866-9_7

source of reflexive analysis or a source of information that is assumed without prior criticism. If the messages we receive through the media are in accordance with those that are transmitted to young generations from an early age, both at home and at school, they are legitimized in such a way that the experiences that contradict them can be considered absurd. Such is the case of gender stereotypes.

Media often persist in representing women, and their relationships with men, in a traditional way; in which stereotypes and hierarchies can be identified from a perspective that is trained in gender violence. These are the ones that either covertly or openly contribute to perpetuating situations of inequality and the prevalence of imbalanced relations between genders; such situations constitute the substratum that favors the manifestation of gendered violence.

The inequalities that are established between men and women on which all the societies that we know are based, reach the highest degree of expression in family contexts and relationship frameworks. Due to the private environments in which these inequalities manifest, it becomes more difficult to identify, legislate or punish them. Moreover, many expressions of violence within a couple, wrapped in the myth of romantic love, are sometimes perceived in Western culture as signs of commitment and infatuation.

Although it is from adolescence when sexual attraction arises with erotic nuances, humans begin to be socialized about love as early as childhood. From the children's tales of princesses awaiting their princes for rescue followed by happily ever after, an education in differentiated roles within the couple relationship begins. Likewise, songs, poems and movies that accompany teenagers and young adults share the same idea with other nuances, and convey the same message. This education on love (sexist and patriarchal) involves almost all people, thus creating conditions that favor women's vulnerability to violence.

Young people's conceptions about love, violence and gender roles are usually the result of a patriarchal gender socialization that legitimizes and misunderstands many violent and unjust acts that occur within the couple. Their naturalization contributes to their perpetuation. When young people have the power to access the media, not as recipients of information, but as creators, they could have a protagonistic role as change agents. For this reason, we explore some conceptions that Journalism students of both sexes at the University of Holguín have about romantic love, gender violence and the conditions sustaining it. Their critical or traditional view of these phenomena will turn them into those who subvert or legitimize male domination.

Gender Violence in Relationships

One of the most commonly used conceptualizations of gender violence is the one stated in Article One of the United Nations Declaration on the Elimination of Violence Against Women of 1993 (p. 2), where gender violence is defined as:

> Any act of violence based on belonging to the female sex that has or may result in physical, sexual or psychological harm or suffering for women, as well as threats of such acts, coercion or arbitrary deprivation of liberty, either occurring in public life or in private.

The concept refers to a wide range of actions that could occur in any context. In this chapter we specifically refer to the violence that occurs against women in the context of heterosexual relationships. Such violence is conditioned by sociocultural constructions related to the fact of being a woman and responds to a structural phenomenon that favors the maintenance of inequality between sexes. It is an exercise of power that perpetuates sexist domination. It is precisely because of this structural nature that domestic violence is much more tolerated and therefore, more widespread than it is often believed.

In Cuba, there is a 'consensus patriarchy' (Fernández, 2005) and the patriarchal ideology that comes with it is in the social imaginary of both men and women. The consensus patriarchy is one where equality between men and women is officially expressed, but in subtle and implicit ways, an androcentric vision of reality that overvalues the masculine and discriminates against women continues to exist. In our opinion,[1] this consensus patriarchy survives and perpetuates itself in Cuban society. In contrast to official communications that declare equality between sexes, from childhood, and throughout life, Cuba keeps a permanent sexist socialization.

The fact that the symbolic subordination that exists by one gender over another is not recognized makes power imbalances between men and women invisible and turns such power imbalances into the fundamental foundations for violent relationships. It is within the couple relationship framework where inequalities are most readily evident, because although public policies in Cuba have significantly stimulated the insertion of women in the public world, there have not been enough efforts to stimulate men to a more responsible family and parental relationship. Moreover, in conjugality, the female body has historically been a space that is subject to control.

The above described situation is an element of vulnerability that leads to the emergence and maintenance of varied manifestations of violence against women, especially in the context of the heterosexual relationship. The ones that most commonly coexist from ignorance and invisibility are the psychological ones, which rest on customs and traditions naturalized by society. Those who attack out of sexist reasons are, in fact, demonstrating behaviors that are considered "normal" and respond, ultimately, to appropriate models for each sex (Orborne, 2009).

The social psychologist Martín Baró[2] claimed that what is considered violent will be so according to the interpretation and assessment made of the violent fact depending on the values and interests that prevail in the society in which it occurs and, under the same principles, it will be subject to censorship or approval (personal communication, October 26, 1987). In patriarchal societies the fact that women are symbolically subordinated to men is naturalized, especially in the context of marriage, which brings about the structuring of an unquestionable belief system that confers the husband the possibility of choosing how to spend time, the participation in the public sphere, the social relations that he establishes, etc., thus forcing his autonomy as a citizen, and creating a distance between formal equality (what is legislated) and substantive or real equality.

On the other hand, there are specific phenomena within the couple relationship that add characteristic peculiarities to this type of violent relationship. In its most general classifications (physical, sexual and psychological), its multiple manifestations take on distinctive nuances due to the fact that the husband from the symbolic perspective, has permissions that a stranger would not have. For example, when the wife is forced to have sexual intercourse by an unknown man, it perceived as and prosecuted as an illegal rape; however, studies carried out with doctors, psychologists and jurists show that there is a certain level of tolerance when the husband is the perpetrator who performs this action (Torralbas, 2014; Torralbas & Calcerrada, 2016).

Another illustrative example of a violent relationship would be when a husband forbids his wife to work or visit family, friends or to attend recreational activities. If a stranger did so, it could be considered a crime against personal liberty covered by the Penal Code, Article 269 (Law 62, 1987). However, it is usually assumed as part of the peculiarities that couples may have when the husband sets prohibitions of this type on his wife's behavior. Although generally speaking, society criticizes these behaviors, they are not perceived as crimes or extraordinary events. The above described situations might suggest that when such interactions occur, the woman willingly remains in the relationship with her husband because she likes the way she is treated. Bourdieu's (2000) analysis of symbolic violence and how the normalization of what is assigned to each gender makes women assume a subordinate role are useful to dismantle this idea. Thus, we elucidate some ways in which the power of cultural influence legitimizes behaviors, positions and even injustices.

From the social imaginary, many myths also accompany the understanding, or rather, misunderstanding of the gender violence phenomenon. Some of those reflected in literature suggest that people involved in violent relationships are "pathological." That is why, if the woman remains in the abusive relationship, she is often labeled as a masochist or as being very weak or insecure. On the other hand, a man who mistreats his partner is ascribed mental problems or being an alcoholic. These conceptions, which exist in Europe, the United States and Latin America, have been refuted by Gender scholars. These authors critique these understandings because they place causality in the individual and do not explore the social and cultural sphere, where much of the motivation lies (Proveyer, 2005).

There is a myth stating that when a woman is mistreated by her husband "she did to something provoke him." It is problematic for a variety of reasons. First, it reflects the (wrong) idea that physical abuse can somehow be justified. In fact, the main risk factor to become a victim of violence is that of being a woman and the sociocultural subordination of her position with respect to men. The tendency to think of violent behavior as something innate, that belongs to the essence of the human being and that men are aggressive by nature is also very common. This is a flawed understanding of violence, however, as it is really a behavior learned in the socialization of gender and in authoritarian sociocultural and power use models, where it is validated as a way to resolve conflicts (Proveyer, 2005).

Nevertheless, there *are* concrete dynamics that occur in violent relationships and contribute to women remaining in such abusive relations.

For example, many battered women manifest so-called "learned helplessness," in which after several unsuccessful attempts to get out of the violent relationship, a woman can lose hope to extricate herself from the violent partnership. Then, although objectively the opportunity of separation arises, passivity and apathy inhibit the action of leaving. This situation is often the result of the lack of social support networks that make the solution viable (Walker, 2009).

Victims of violence are also described to experience fear, a sensation that brings about paralyzing effects and makes one believe in the omnipotence of the victimizer. The idea that the aggressor is capable of knowing everything, being everywhere and fulfilling all his threats makes the victim feel more vulnerable. Fear can be of physical aggression or of any situation that could generate conflicts that trigger abuse, leading her to behave in a way that pleases the husband. The fear of facing him is in the self-perception of weakness.

Known as the battered woman syndrome, its main features include: the woman thinks the violence she is experiencing is her fault, and she becomes unable to place the responsibility of violence elsewhere. In addition, she fears for her life and/or that of her children, and she has the irrational idea that the abuser is omnipresent and omniscient: he can be anywhere and know what happens or could happen in her life. This syndrome is associated with post-traumatic stress disorder and therefore it becomes very difficult for women to leave the situation of abuse on their own (Walker, 2009).

Another factor that contributes to the occurrence and maintenance of such violent relationships, and therefore to the perpetuation of violence, is the isolation to which women victims of abuse are surreptitiously subjected. Isolation consists on getting women away, either gradually or completely, from any type of social interaction that may include prohibition of working outside the home and physically distancing her from family and friends. This situation creates a greater state of vulnerability and therefore reinforces the arrogance of the victimizer, thus creating a vicious circle.

All the previously described phenomena are elements that help us understand the complexity that a battered woman lives. This situation has multiple social, cultural and psychological conditions that sustain it. Bearing in mind that coexistence with gender violence is an everyday life issue, which is learned from parents, strengthened in the media and subtly maintained in schools, it is not surprising that the majority of influential spaces in our lives, like family and work environments, become violence reproducers and legitimizers. Deepening our understanding of gender-based violence against women in couples relationships must become a mandatory task of all those professionals committed to social justice and especially those with a greater share of power to achieve such justice.

Young Men and Women in Relationships

University students of both sexes are in a moment of life where they begin to be autonomous in relation to the family, although in most cases their student status would still make them financially dependent on their parents. It is a moment of transit where their objective conditions of life are interrelated with new psychological formations that are consolidated in young people, to give rise to a peculiar circumstance where dependence and independence are interconnected.

When talking about youth in Cuba, reference is made to the population segments between 14 and 30 years of age, in accordance with the Childhood and Youth Code currently in force in the country. Three age groups can be distinguished: *early youth* or adolescence—between 14 and 17 years old, *middle youth*—between 18 and 24 years old—that forms the central core of youth, and *mature* or late youth—between 25 and 30 years old. For our present research, we chose the middle youth age range for our sample. We place importance on this group because that is when the conception of the world is consolidated. Psychological training allows young people to develop their own criteria about their reality with which they feel emotionally engaged and become effective regulators of their behavior. It is this condition that allows personality self-determination, that is, the possibility of acting reflexively with relative independence from external influences (Domínguez, 2003; Domínguez et al., 2014).

Unlike adolescents, who are more likely to find shallower and weaker relationships, the relations young people in the middle age range of both sexes begin to build usually gain stability and commitment. For the latter, professional motivations and love interests are two great pillars on which their development is based. This characteristic is still tinged by the concrete conditions of life in Cuba, where the demands of the labor market or the search for better work and earning opportunities make it more complex to reconcile personal and couple-family-work life (Arés, 2018).

In twenty-first century Cuba, life as a couple goes through important challenges ranging from the material and economic conditions to the demands that generate satisfaction and emotional well-being in the intersubjective sphere. Although all this has led to high divorce rates, research shows that many Cubans continue to desire to live as a couple. This speaks more to a crisis between the type of relationship we form according to the acquired socially acceptable models and to the type of relationships we aspire to have than to a generalized relationship crisis per se (Arés, 2002). That is, it is still an aspiration to live in union with a partner, however, there is a requirement that the quality of the relationship justifies its stability and maintenance. Increasingly, the subordinate and unequal relationships that characterized couples from previous generations are less acceptable.

Love bond is structured depending on how gender roles are expressed in relationships. Many times the *romantic love myth* plays an important role in defining such bond (Fernández, 2006). Romantic love as an ideal arises in modernity when the possibility of forming a couple motivated by affections and not by political, economic or class interests appears. This romantic love is inoculated from childhood through children's tales of passive princesses that depend on princes, whose mission in life is to be beautiful and please their princes, and the sign of success is getting married. Adolescence is usually accompanied by romantic songs with lyrics like "I would leave everything if you stayed," "I give you my life" and "you are my life" that shape the idea that any sacrifice for love is valid, that not having a partner translates to being alone and the expression of a woman's success is to achieve a good marriage. Romantic movies and current soap operas reinforce these same ideas to a greater or lesser extent, where the sexist distribution of domestic roles and the overload of female roles are also reproduced and naturalized.

As pointed out by Giddens (1998), romantic love implies the idea of equality because it assumes that a relationship can be derived from the emotional involvement of two individuals rather than from external social criteria. Romantic love, however, is deeply distorted in terms of power, because the double sexual morality means it is experienced differently by men and women. Therefore, under the idea that everything can be achieved in the name of love, that love implies sacrifice and surrender (usually not in the same way for both members of the couple), dreams of romantic love have often led women to an irksome domestic subjection.

It is usually the space of the relationship where the woman lives the greatest conflict between what is assigned and what is taken on. Cuban women, after the 1959 Revolution, have been challenged to be competent in the public sphere while still being treated in traditional ways within the domestic space. Home maintenance, caring for the children and tending to the husband's needs are still part of the expectations of their performance. Becoming a being for another being as the core of female identity continues to exist. To be able to reconcile these responsibilities that accommodate the lives of others is seen as proof of love and part of the sacrifices that love imposes on women. This was reflected in an investigation carried out in the province of Holguín with married couples that shared the same profession for approximately the same amount of time. Results showed that regardless of how much both members of the couple financially contributed to the household, the woman was still the one with less leisure time for herself and the one who was most involved in domestic responsibilities (Lam, 2012). These data matched up with those from the National Survey of Gender Equality that showed that in a week Cuban women spend, on average, 14 more hours on unpaid work than men (Alvares et al., 2018).

For young people, who usually aspire to consolidate or start a relationship, romantic love becomes a central and structuring element of such relationship. However, this is one of the social axes that articulates women's vulnerability, since it makes them docile, willing and prone to sacrifice (Fernández, 2005). Love is also a sociocultural fact; you learn to love, but, who teaches it? Only a critical look could allow new forms of love to be constructed; more equitable, respectful and empathic ones. In this endeavor, mass media that has been made by young people and for young people plays a critical role.

Media as a Space for Gender Socialization

For Coral López (2007), mass media (including new technologies) constitute, in most cases, the ideological instruments of patriarchal society, double morality and neoliberal economy, due to the great influence they exert on values, customs and life models of men and women. The Cuban state does not fail to recognize this power and, for this reason, since the National Follow-up Action Plan to the Beijing Conference, which came into effect in May 1997, a section is dedicated to women and the media. In this plan, measures are proposed either to empower women in this environment or to train the staff to achieve audiovisual journalistic products supported by awareness and training in gender topics (FMC, 1999).

However, coinciding with the Cuban feminist Lirians Gordillo (2018), a reporter for the Women's News Service of Latin America and the Caribbean, spaces for debate on gender and feminism are still scarce on the island. For her, it is important to identify the three fundamental directions when dealing with gender violence. First of all: to recognize the Communication System as a subsystem within the Patriarchal System that reproduces and justifies patriarchal violence through chauvinistic imaginary. Second: to identify the symbolic violence that the media exerts in the context where they broadcast information. And third: to exploit the potential of communication to denounce, raise awareness, convene and generate new meanings.

The journalist delves into everyday life to build the social stories that, beyond their informative intention, generate a symbolic universe, legitimize beliefs, reaffirm myths and offer meaning to everyday life. As stated by Cuban researcher Isabel Moya (2010), media stories are transcendental in shaping the myths of our day and they constitute stages for the dramatization of the world. Therefore, he who exercises journalism, as an activist of ideas, has a transcendental role to transform social conceptions that limit the full freedom of human beings and to dismantle beliefs that have historically been naturalized as absolute truths from his communicative ability.

Among the arbitrary conceptions established in modern societies are the essentialist positions that reaffirm a duty as being feminine and masculine. Media constantly reproduce stereotyped images of gender identities, thus continuing to trap, from that space of symbolic domain, the human being in molds that hinder their development. What would foster change would be to approach reality with a critical eye that reveals human relationships in their complexity and, above all, shows us a world marked by power relations: we live in a patriarchal society where gender inequalities prevail.

The reproduction of sexism in the media through language, content and images originated in the survival of conceptions and traditions that prevail and settle in the culture of inequality. Therefore, the journalist can use these same resources to generate countercurrent speeches and representations that reveal and denounce the existence of an ideology that underpins gender inequalities (Moya, 2010). An inclusive language should be used in media. What is not named is inexistent. Mentioning feminine and masculine is a political position. Also, when using language, it is important to mind the way in which adjectives are used to refer to men, women, girls and boys in order to avoid qualifiers that reinforce gender stereotypes.

In many countries, ethical management of news about the murder of women becomes a major challenge (Sánchez, 2008) because the way they are treated often places women in a position of re-victimization. Although such news is not used to create sensationalism or to increase the audience rating in Cuban media. Nevertheless the Cuban case reveals another dynamic: since news about the murder of women is not publicized, it could generate the impression among the population that it does not exist. Therefore, due to the power of media to make things visible and denounce realities, the counterpart to a yellow press could be a long-form journalism and social denunciation supported by a scientific bibliography, reliable statistics and the recommendations of specialists. That type of work does not abound in the Cuban press or television, thus generating the illusion that violent crime is a rare or minor problem.

Undoubtedly, reflective, deep and committed analysis would only be achieved with a discourse constructed from a gender perspective, which allows us to visualize and recognize the existence of hierarchy and inequal relations between men and women, expressed in the subordination and discrimination toward women in the organization of societies (Lagarde, 1996). Assuming a gender perspective requires education and awareness in this area. It may be that a journalism student of either sex, just for complying with the requirements of a syllabus, is able to reproduce the fundamental concepts and assumptions of Gender Theory, but if he or she fails to get emotionally involved and adopt a position in this regard, he or she could unlikely become an agent of change and social progress with his or her actions. On the other hand, if this professional achieves awareness of the subject and assumes the struggles to claim the place of women and social minorities as his or her own, but without having a foundation in gender training that allows a critical look of reality, guided by good intentions, he or she could be re-victimizing or reproducing gender stereotypes through his or her speech that would only contribute to maintaining the *status quo*.

Based on all the above, as researchers, we proposed our project to better understand what current/contemporary students of both sexes think about gender violence against women within the couple relationship. Specifically, we wanted to understand the conceptions of journalism students because of the important role they may play in the future for perpetuating or changing ideas and standards in Cuban society, if they have achieved enough education and awareness to overcome prejudices, discriminations and manifestations of symbolic violence that currently continue to be real and negative in twenty-first century Cuba.

Hereinafter, we describe the journalism major (*carrera*) at the University of Holguín to establish the academic base on which students are preparing to become journalists. Then, we analyze and reflect on the results and close with some observations for the future.

Empirical Results and Reflections

The degree in Journalism at the University of Holguín began in 2006, with eight graduations through Spring 2019. The degree is governed by Study Plan D, in force since 2008 (MES, 2008), which stipulates that its duration is five school years, composed of ten semesters, of which nine are curricular and the last one is dedicated to the culminating capstone project. This curriculum used to have a subject, in the final year, that dealt with different issues associated with professional practice and had the possibility of including a topic on gender, however, it was removed in 2017 to give space to other seemingly more urgent issues. For this reason, in recent years the subject of domestic violence has not been discussed in Journalism classes.[3] This means that graduates in Journalism from the University of Holguín treat topics related to gender violence within a couple based on lessons learned that have become "common sense" acquired during their gender socialization throughout their lives. The decision to remove the specific treatment of these topics in the curriculum motivated the present investigation, exploring the conceptions that future journalists of both sexes in the province of Holguín have in relation to issues that serve as pillars to the conditions that favor gender violence.

To obtain information on conceptions of gender violence and associated phenomena, we prepared a survey that we administered in March 2019. The surveyed sample was composed of all fourth and fifth year (the last two years of the journalism course) male and female students. Fifth year students have already finished the curricular part of the degree and the fourth year students have only two semesters of classes remaining during which no topic related to gender will be addressed. The study group, (relatively small, but including all students enrolled in these courses) was made up of twelve young people, four of them in fourth year and eight in the fifth. Of these, two were men and ten were women, between 21 and 24 years of age.

When asked if all the same possibilities of well-being and development exist for men and women in our society, a little more than half, (seven students, one of them male) considered it to be true. In our opinion, the fact that legislatively speaking there are no differences between men and women, together with the lack of education in gender perspective, causes the illusion that both are equal. In general, in post-graduate studies, management posts or any position that is considered successful, women tend to combine their professional life with home and family care, however, the male experience in obtaining these same achievements, is usually backed by a woman (wife or mother) who, from the domestic sphere, makes the path easier.

On the other hand, given the illusion of equality, a woman who does not achieve the socially expected development usually perceives it as a personal disability, not related to the sociocultural context that fosters it. In Cuban media, this is one of the ideas that is most frequently exposed, and every time it is done without due feminist analysis, it contributes to making inequality invisible and in doing, perpetuating it. Only a trained look on gender issues could reveal that the amount of women in Parliament or in management positions does not matter if they do not have a gender focus on their practices and ideas. In the long run, Cuban women are educated to become what gender theorists of both sexes call super woman syndrome (Friedan, 1983), i.e., the aspiration or demand of the woman who is successful as a professional, a mother and a housewife. Of course, such success in all spheres is accompanied by a high cost in physical and emotional health.

Four students answer that it is false that in our society the same possibilities of well-being and development exist for men and women. The only respondent who claimed not to know stated that, "*legally yes, but socially not so much.*" This is an example of the contradiction between what is officially declared and what results from daily experience, as equal laws are not enough to achieve equality. Only by recognizing the sociocultural differences and disadvantages between the sexes is it possible to work with equitable approaches that achieve fairer relationships and conditions for both sexes.

When inquiring about the causes of violence against women within couples relationships—specifically if they are based on a low level of culture and alcoholism—seven students (one of them male) consider it true; three answered 'I don't know.' This suggests that most students have internalized the previously explained myth about the relationship between these factors and violence in couples. None of the surveyed individuals recognized the causes that have been proven by the social sciences: the power imbalance between the sexes and the patriarchal mandate that concedes men domain over women. Only one respondent—male—reports that it is false, claiming that "... *any professional can commit this type of grievance.*" This answer suggests that, at least, the respondent recognized that domestic violence is not a phenomenon exclusive of people of low cultural level, but it does not necessarily demonstrate an understanding of the complexity of the issue.

This is the reason for our concern about the education and awareness of journalists regarding a gender perspective. If they place emphasis on elements such as alcohol, cultural level or other individual causes without delving into the sociocultural origins of the phenomenon in their journalistic work, the opportunity to denounce and raise awareness of the need for cultural and institutional change that perpetuates violence is lost. A look, from a gender perspective, to school institutions, family, laws, communication products, among others, would reveal their role by naturalizing the subordination of women.

As to the legal instruments available to women in Cuba in order to access help in the case of being mistreated, four students declared that it was false; one of them—male—claimed that "... *only physical violence is protected.*" Although not explicitly stated, the student's assertion shows a recognition that there are several types of violence—that is, psychological, verbal, emotional—that are even more invisible but sometimes even more insidious than physical violence. Notably, another student—female—expresses her solid disagreement over the inadequacy of laws and denouncing mechanisms. For her, the matter is even more important and frustrating because harassment in public spaces is carried out with total impunity for the aggressor.

From the two students—one female and the other male, who responded 'I don't know,' we can also glean some insights from a gender perspective into education and awareness in their future work in media. For example, the man comments that "*there are surely laws regulating the subject*," which indicates his ignorance of the subject, thus reflecting the lack of importance or relevance for him in his daily life. It is curious, in addition, that he chooses to assume that there is protection, counting on the existing legal system to protect the vulnerabilities of women in society. On the other hand, the female student's ignorance could suggest several interpretations, including: she has not made the effort to inquire about a situation in which she could also be involved; or gender violence has not directly affected her life and/or she does not realize that, for gender violence, the greatest risk factor is just being a woman.

Even more striking are the responses of six female students who consider that there is enough legal protection. This answer is not surprising, since it coincides with a response found in the National Survey on Gender Equality, which reflects that:

> 88.7% of the Cuban population aged 15 to 74 considers that the laws that protect women are applied in Cuba and that there are specific policies and actions in favor of them. 85.5% of people also state that there are places or services that provide attention to women who are victims of violence and 83.7% that there are organizations where women can raise their needs and concerns. (Alvares et al., 2018: 23)

Beyond the limitations of this survey that inquires about the existence of aid resources and not about its efficiency or quality, it shows the perception of the vast majority of respondents concerning the existence of laws and places to help battered women. These six female students not only reflect and share the general opinion of Cubans from both sexes, but also take it for granted without expressing doubts or skepticism, and without analytically reflecting on the subject. Since these future journalists do not to have a critical view, formed in a gender perspective, they would be reproducers and legitimizers in their communicative works of some of the situations of violence and injustice that Cuban women will experience in the future.

It is important to clarify the legal and social realities regarding violence against women in Cuba in the twenty-first century. Under the principle of equality, there is no specific law against gender or domestic violence in Cuba; instead, this issue is processed in a general law that equally judges the violence exerted by men toward women and vice versa. And as "most of the ways of understanding equality are paradoxically discriminatory" (Avila, 2012: 20), when judging those who are unequal as equal, the disadvantages and inequities continue to be perpetuated. However, even if there were a law, it would not be enough to sufficiently and efficiently protect battered women due to the fact that the execution of what is prescribed in law implies the written law as such, as well as the knowledge, attitudes and uses that the operator of such law can make, who usually has a limited understanding of the phenomenon (Torralbas, 2014).

In Cuba there are no shelters for battered women in the face of extreme danger in a domestic relationship; instead, women must go to the home of relatives or friends as they do not have an institutional alternative. Moreover, in circumstances where the need to report a case of rape arises, it has to be done under the same conditions of lack of privacy as a common crime. There are no police stations or places where formally comprehensive attention is given to battered women, whether from the legal sphere or from the medical one. Options promoted by national television, such as the facilities for specialized assistance for abused women, consist of consultations offered by the House of Orientation to Women and Family, a project sponsored by the Federation of Cuban Women (the only female institution in the country whose objective is to achieve full equality for women and promote social change accordingly). However, this consultancy works with professionals from other institutions, such as the Public Health Ministry, Ministry of Education and Ministry of Justice, whose presence and participation could undermine the domestic violence professionals' ability to tend to the immediate emotional and psychological needs of the victims.

Given this situation, to think that there is enough protection for battered women shows, beyond the lack of legal culture, how far the female students in our study are from the knowledge or understanding of the needs of an abused woman. Likewise, there is so much naturalization of the societal disadvantages of women and the invisibility of their vulnerabilities that there is no criticism of the institutional shortages that perpetuate and prolong these inadequacies.

Nine out of twelve participants consider violence against women as a significant social problem in Cuba. This suggests a certain sensitivity to the problem; at least they consider this issue as important enough to be taken into account. On the other hand, none of the respondents provided any deep explanation or assessment of the phenomenon, suggesting a superficial exposure to or concern for the matter. Another research participant does not consider violence a significant social problem, and the remaining two respondents 'don't know.' The fact that not everyone recognizes it as a significant social problem may reflect the problem mentioned above: the *status quo* of attitudes and behaviors regarding violence against women is perpetuated by patriarchal systems—of media, education, and public health—that employ staff that is untrained in a gender perspective. As such, the phenomenon receives insufficient attention, either by way of statistics or by social criticism, in Cuba. In fact, there are no public statistics on the number of battered women or of those seeking help for this reason, and the matter is only made visible publicly, off the record, after a woman has been killed by her partner.

Nevertheless, the fact that most of the students consider violence a significant social fact is a sign that it is beginning to appear on the public agenda. This contrasts with our own personal experiences 15 years ago, in the first decade of this century, when talking about violence against women, even in the academic environment of the Universidad de Holguín, generated resistance as it was considered non-existent.

When inquiring about the quality of the media's treatment of violence against women, i.e., if it is deep and committed, ten students think otherwise, perceiving a lack of treatment of the issue in media. They expressed themselves with the following opinions:

- The treatment is usually propagandist and insufficient.
- Cuban soap operas are chauvinistic.
- It is not usually a priority and few publishers deal with it.
- Data are missing, figures of victims of violence, specialists' interviews, hearing testimonials from real victims. Many times the information ends up by giving a 'teque[4]' ... that is absolutely not committed to the matter.

We suggest that both media and journalists, of both sexes, who sporadically deal with the topic of domestic violence are based on superficial and stereotyped information and knowledge about the phenomenon. On the other hand, it appears that this problem has been undervalued and mishandled in the country's political agenda, perhaps because this problem is considered to have been already overcome by the Cuban revolutionary government.

As for romantic love, seven students consider it 'false' that the strength of a woman's love can stop a man from being violent. In their comments on this question, the majority of respondents claimed that a violent man needs "therapy," "specialized help," and "it is due to the personality of the perpetrator." All their answers revolved around seeing the abuser as a pathological person who needs help and that love alone cannot cause change. At the same time, it was surprising to us that even five young people (four females and one male) considered that the force of love would change the behavior of an abusive man, suggesting the health of the myth that 'love can overcome anything' in today's society. Given the double sexual morality of Cuban society, the same sacrifice for love cannot be expected from men and women equally. It is women, responding to the structuring of a feminine identity educated to become beings for others, from whom commitment is expected for the benefit of others. Using love as an excuse is also a subtle way to justify the sacrifice and submission of women.

Looking at the group as a whole, it is evident that the students have a sensitivity to the problem of domestic abuse as most of them expressed that it is a social problem, and that it is not treated with enough depth and commitment in the media. This suggests that these students perceive the lack of a deep and reflective treatment on the domestic problem in media. However, their knowledge suggests that when they are the ones who develop communicative materials as journalistic professionals, perhaps they will continue to reproduce this same situation that they now criticize. That is, the opinions and attitudes of the students do not reflect education and awareness in a gender perspective, therefore they do not have a sufficiently critical understanding of the phenomenon. If the belief—not instructed or informed—that men and women have equal conditions for their development persists, the absence of continuous struggles for equality could be justified because it has allegedly already been achieved. This is precisely how the *status quo* is reproduced in terms of domestic violence.

Misconceptions also persist on the causes of violence within couples, relating them to low cultural level and alcoholism. Journalistic works focused on these elements as a cause only help to increase the already invisible way in which all socializing agents, such as school, family and of course, the media, among others, contribute to naturalizing the male domination that is culturally instilled, which is ultimately what causes violence within the relationship. The myth of romantic love, which is obviously still healthy within our sample of students, reinforces these conditions, without creating positive changes in terms of the social and legal equality of battered women or the reduction of violence.

Finally, we emphasize the fact that the prevailing ignorance over the existence of spaces of protection for abused women or not is truly striking, when domestic violence is a problem that could involve anyone, not only from the professional position but also from the personal one. We fear that our respondents' future journalistic work and influence in the media will not be used to raise awareness about these shortages in Cuban society or to promote a change of this social reality.

Conclusion

In the present treatment of the perceptions that these male and female Journalism students of the University of Holguín have about violence against women, it is evident that there is still a misunderstanding of the phenomenon in this generation of Cuban youth. Their answers to the questionnaire point to the lack of social criticism and analysis of the socio-cultural conditions that give rise to it. In our opinion, this constitutes conditions to foster training spaces in gender issues for students of journalism students, because in contrast to the importance that they give to this issue, there is evidence of lack of preparation to practice a journalism that is really a space for social critique and transformation. Cuban television and radio could become privileged spaces to contribute to truly informed awareness of the violence in couples relationships from a gender perspective.

Taking into account the power of media and to build imaginaries and legitimize realities, the Cuban feminist agenda must be considered among its most pressing priorities, to stimulate government policies that favor journalists and communicators education in gender issues through a gender perspective. Committed journalism can only be accompanied by a solid formation and a specific sensitization that help to dismantle erroneous beliefs, or else there is a risk of reinforcing them. We are only at the beginning of the road. There is still much left to do.

Notes

1. The experience of more than ten years of one of the authors as an academic and researcher of the subject and her systematic participation in the main events of the country related to Gender Studies, inform her statements above.
2. Martín Baró was a Spanish social psychologist based in Costa Rica, founder of the psychology of liberation, an indispensable author in social critical psychology. The reference is to the original manuscript

of the conference that the author presented at the University of Costa Rica during the Second Event of Social Psychology, on October 26, 1987, whose title was Violence in Central America: a psychosocial vision.

3. Interview conducted on March 15, 2019 with M.Sc. Ivonne Pérez Pérez, who from 2016 to the present has served as Coordinator of the Bachelor's degree in Journalism at the University of Holguín. She belongs to the first graduating class in Journalism from the university, and since then she has also been a professor in the major.
4. *Teque* is a popular word that means empty and baseless speech.

Bibliography

Alvares, M., Franco, M., Palermo, Y., Iglesias, M., & Díaz, Y. (2018). *Encuesta Nacional sobre la Igualdad de Género*. ONIG-2016. Informe de resultados. Editorial de la Mujer. Acceso http://www.one.cu/enig2016.htm

Arés, P. (2002). *Psicología de la familia. Una aproximación a su estudio*. Editorial Universitaria Félix Varela.

Arés, P. (2018). *Individuo, familia, sociedad. El desafío de ser feliz*. Editorial Caminos.

Ávila, R. (2012). Género, derecho y discriminación. ¿Una mirada masculina? In Y. González (Ed.), *Las expresiones del género en el derecho y sus expresiones en la legislación y en la práctica jurídica* (pp. 3–39). Unión Nacional de Jurista de Cuba. Acceso: http://www.unjc.co.cu

Bourdieu, P. (2000). *La dominación masculina*. Editorial Anagrama.

Domínguez, L. (2003). Características de diferentes etapas en el desarrollo de la personalidad. In R. Castellanos (Ed.), *Psicología. Selección de textos* (pp. 59–89). Editorial Universitaria Félix Varela.

Domínguez, M. I., Rego, I., & Castilla, C. (2014). *Socialización de adolescentes y jóvenes. Retos y oportunidades para la sociedad cubana actual*. Editorial de Ciencias Sociales.

Fernández, L. (2005). Género y Subjetividad. *Pensando en la Personalidad* (Vol. 2, pp. 150–168). Editorial Universitaria Félix Varela.

Fernández, L. (2006). *Personalidad y Relaciones de Pareja*. Editorial Universitaria Félix Varela.

FMC: Federación de Mujeres Cubanas. (1999). *Plan de Acción Nacional de la República de Cuba de seguimiento a la IV Conferencia de la ONU sobre la mujer*. Editorial de la Mujer.

Friedan, B. (1983). *La segunda fase*. Plaza & Janés.

Giddens, A. (1998). *La transformación de la intimidad. Sexualidad, amor y erotismo en las sociedades modernas*. Ediciones Cátedra.

Gordillo, L. (2018). *Una postura incómoda: crítica feminista y medios de comunicación*. SEMlac XIII (10). Acceso: http://redsemlac-cuba.net/archivo/Comunicacion/Documentos/

Lagarde, M. (1996) La perspectiva de género. In *Género y feminismo. Desarrollo humano y democracia* (pp. 13–38). Editorial. horas y HORAS.

Lam, C. (2012). *Micropoderes en tres parejas de profesionales del municipio Holguín* (unpublished undergraduate thesis). Universidad de Holguín.

Ley No 62 Código Penal, Capítulo I, Sección primera, Artículo 279. (1987).

López, C. (2007). Ideología, medios de comunicación y género. *Comunicación e Cidadanía, 1*, 101–106.

MES: Ministerio de Educación Superior. (2008). *Carrera de Periodismo. Plan de Estudios "D"*. Universidad de La Habana, Cuba.

Moya, I. (2010). *El sexo de los ángeles. Una mirada de género a los medios de comunicación*. Publicaciones Acuario.

Osborne, R. (2009). *Apuntes sobre violencia de género*. Edicions Bellaterra.

Proveyer, C. (2005). La violencia contra la mujer en las relaciones de pareja. Consideraciones para su estudio. In C. Proveyer (Ed.), *Selección de lecturas de Sociología Política Social de Género* (pp. 132–172). Editorial Universitaria Félix Varela.

Sánchez, G. (2008). Violencia machista y medios de comunicación. El tratamiento informativo de los delitos relacionados con el maltrato a mujeres. *Revista Comunicación y Hombre, 4*, 3–14.

Torralbas, A. (2014). *Saberes y vivencias del jurista penalista sobre la violencia de género contra la mujer en la relación conyugal* (unpublished Master's thesis). Universidad de La Habana.

Torralbas, A., & Calcerrada, M. (2016). Using Primary care to address violence against women in intimate partner relationships. *MEDICC Review, 18*(4), 38–42.

United Nations. (1993). *Declaración sobre la eliminación de la violencia contra la mujer*.

Walker, L. E. A. (2009). *The battered woman Syndrome* (3rd ed.). Springer.

CHAPTER 8

Youth with Existential Crises: A Transdisciplinary View for Comprehension and Intervention

Lisbet Almaguer Sao

Introduction

At present, the formation of values in youth constitutes a subject of interest theoretically, empirically and methodologically in the social sciences. Promoting its development reveals a highly complex training mission in today's reality. At a global level, some of the problems experienced by young people can be identified: increase in unemployment; psychological disorders such as panic attacks, drug addiction, depression, suicidal ideation, eating disorders; exercise of prostitution; as well as existential emptiness.

This chapter was translated by Richard N. Gioioso with the help of William Pinkow '24, Saint Joseph's University

L. A. Sao (✉)
Department of Psychology, Universidad de Holguín, Holguín, Cuba

R. N. Gioioso et al. (eds.), *Youth and Development in Cuba*,
https://doi.org/10.1007/978-3-030-90866-9_8

Research on youth worldwide emphasizes the need to stimulate their development due to the process of consolidation of personality and its impact on an intrapersonal, group and social level. It includes their searches and projections, the uncertainties arising from changes in social thought, and the reformulation of symbolic representations in times of contradictions and conflicts with themselves, with others, and those of the environment. These issues constitute the object of contemporary psychological, sociological, axiological and pedagogical research.

Research in this regard has been carried out in Latin America. Moral and Ovejero (2004) studied young pre-adults as social adolescents, who are going through a crisis, the etiology of which does not rest solely on their internal conditions. Individualizing, and even pathologizing, the problems of post-adolescents represents an exercise through which, by unlinking each case from its multidimensional determinants, the responsibility of other agencies and powers involved at the social, family, academic, media and institutional levels is intentionally reduced.

Agulló and Ovejero (2001) considered that "diseases" or alterations in the way of being in the world have always existed, but the disproportionate increase in the current incidence rightly suggests that there is a strong social component. Analytically, I would frame them within what has been called "social neurosis" or "mass neurosis." According to Viktor E. Frankl (1980), these moments of crisis are characterized by the inability to find meaning in life, by the presence of existential emptiness and reduced world projects. Urra (2004), in his characterization of problems of youth in Mexico, argues that in moments of massive disappointment, some young people with fear of freedom, console themselves with discouragement either with various over-activations, through automatic conformity or by redefining fuzzy identities. In his assessment, contemporary youth experience feelings of disappointment, even though they are masked under an appearance of conformity and superficial enjoyment in the form of consumption or youth weekend leisure, as an attempt at non-traumatic adaptation to a reality that is being simulated. In this sense, he expressed: "vitality, effervescence, illusion, sadness and even despair define a stage where the clothes that are worn, the fashions and the ephemeral myths take on an unusual value" (11). Comas et al. (2003) suggest that in recent decades the changes that have occurred, both socioeconomic and cultural, have affected the entire social structure. These transformations cause various references of life to be upset, with which it is necessary to analyze, from a broad perspective, how these changes affect different social strata, especially adolescents and young people and their lifestyles.

Despite efforts to maintain a social project based on socialist morality, Cuban society is not exempt from the impact of the neoliberal crisis of modern times. Cuban young people suffer from problems similar to those that occur in other contexts, with idiosyncratic socioeconomic and spiritual conditions. In Cuba, statistics on mental health from 2000 and 2017 describe the high prevalence of depression and neurotic disorders in adolescents, youth and young adults. Research to determine the causes of this phenomenon and its intervention emphasized the need to promote interdisciplinary practices with emphasis on the formation of values. A symptom that is repeated in the clinical picture of these subjects is the crisis or existential emptiness, expressed as: sadness, anguish, tiredness, boredom, frustration, pessimism, anorexia, fear of death, loss, isolation, phobias, among others.

These signs and symptoms in young people today have a multicausal origin. However, the influence of epochal problems, given at a global level, and their particular impact on the community, the family and individuals is undeniable. An example of the above is the universal expansion of a cultural model that nullifies human differences and standardizes cultural guidelines and practices; diffusion of unique, reductionist forms of thought and language that homogenize the human condition and identity and nullify its diversity. The accentuated aestheticization of human life, which in young people manifests in non-conformity or non-acceptance of their body image, can leads some to start using substances such as steroids to shape their bodies. In other cases, the inadequacy in their self-assessment determines the ingestion of psychoactive substances—stimulants or disinhibitors—as means to achieve individual goals, needs and purposes.

Another of these problems is the dehistoricization of human life projects and their meaning, which can be expressed in a tendency toward existential presentism: "living today as the last day," the "here and now," the division between "virtual life and real life." The latter constitutes an expression of the existential alienation which some young people reach. The disagreement with the real conditions of existence and its contradiction with the desired ones; the inability to restructure life projects or consider other ones; the cancellation of coping styles in the face of conflicts and frustrations become conditioning factors of existential crisis that can lead to the consumption of toxic substances. Its effects can generate: disinhibition, release of endorphins (substances of joy and euphoria), escapism or evasion, among others. These defensive mechanisms try to protect the human conscience from the experiences of psychological pain, but they do not help solve the crisis.

The analysis and assessment of the above information has allowed me to deepen my practice of clinical psychology with many young people experiencing the problems described above. The psychological evaluation I carried out allowed me to characterize the experiences reported by these young subjects: apathy; future uncertainty, pessimism, dichotomous positions on relationships with oneself and with society; and the lack of perseverance in the planning and execution of life projects and panic attacks.

My analysis of the symptoms allowed me to identify the following causes:

- Limited perseverance in planning and achieving goals determined by disagreements between having and being.
- Experiences of future uncertainty, mourning, separation anxiety due to family dispersion caused by emigration.
- Tendencies to escapism expressed in the need to live in other countries as a solution to personal and family problems.
- Poverty in the conceptualization of values such as honesty toward oneself and others, sincerity, truth and authenticity.
- Insufficient independence and personal elaboration of concepts, judgments, evaluations, criteria and beliefs, considered contents of the conception of the world or philosophy of life, as a configuration of the personality.

In my psychological interventions with some of these young people, I was able to verify in them the restoration of the biopsychosocial and spiritual balance. One of the contents of the personality that was enhanced through therapy was the conception of the world, especially in the areas of conflict and frustration: family, sexual, school, work and personal. The change of conceptions, evaluations and judgments about the conditions of the conflictive situation contributed to an improvement in their emotional well-being. In a post-mortem evaluation of the orientation actions I used, I concluded that although I had designed my interventions using the theoretical-methodological foundations of Psychology and axiological and literary resources, they still did not reflect the complexity of the relationship of the general, the particular and the singular in the expression of the phenomenon addressed. Therefore, those interventions would not be efficient to treat other patients. In this sense, a Psychological Orientation Program with an axiological approach was proposed aimed at developing the conception of the world in young people with experiences of existential crisis.

From this perspective, foundations from related social sciences are assumed to achieve the objective of this inquiry—the study of values: their nature, structure, functioning, hierarchy. In addition to this, I included theoretical assumptions about the meaning of life and the existential crisis experienced in young people. Students of values, such as Fernando González Rey (1998), recognize that this issue has been theoretically addressed by Philosophy and Ethics. In an empirical direction, they have been the subject of research by social sciences, such as Psychology, Sociology and Anthropology. Values exist as subjective expressions of the evaluative dimension of the individual, who in her condition of subject is the bearer of her subjective configuration in the personality and the intentional conductor of her expression. The subjective configuration of values is characterized by the integration of the cognitive and the affective, a unit that is expressed in the articulation of the dynamic elements that are structured in their conformation, while their intentional expression occurs through the conscious representations that the subject builds on them.

Values have a social determination as products of the socialization process, so that every society expresses a system of declared values, those that respond to its political-social organization and the ideological forms in which it is represented. Valuable things have always existed for the human being: good, truth, beauty, happiness, virtue. However, the criteria for giving them value has varied over time. For example, their value can be decided according to aesthetic criteria, social schemes, customs, ethical principles or, in other terms, by cost, utility, well-being, pleasure, prestige.

For the purposes of this research, I use axiological, sociological and psychological dimensions of the formation of values as theoretical-methodological foundations of his proposal. Regarding the particular and the singular, I focus my attention on the formation of values in youth, specifically in those young people who experience existential crisis, José Ramón Fabelo Corzo (1989, 2003) has provided critical views on the classic axiological approach to the problem of the nature of values. His proposal recognizes the existence of three fundamental dimensions for values that correspond, in turn, to three levels of analysis of this category. He conceptually distinguishes these dimensions as objective, subjective and instituted and through them gives space to the different particular manifestations of values. I assume this approach for the theoretical and methodological foundation of its axiological alternative. To do this, I address the characterization of the planes of analysis of Fabelo Corzo's values.

The first of these planes allows us to understand values as a constitutive part of social reality itself, as a relationship of significance between the different processes or events of social life and the needs and interests of society as a whole. Each object, phenomenon, event, each result of human activity, performs a certain function in society, acquires one or another social significance, favors or hinders the progressive development of society and, in this sense, is a value or an anti-value. The objective system of values is independent of the appreciation that one has of it, but it is also dynamic, changing, attached to historical-concrete conditions. It is possible that what is considered valuable in the present will not be considered so in the future, because the functional relationship between the subject and the object may have changed.[1]

The second level of analysis refers to the way in which that social significance, which constitutes the objective value, is reflected in individual or collective consciousness. Depending on tastes, aspirations, desires, needs, interests and ideals, each social subject values reality in a specific way. As a result of this evaluation process, he or she forms his or her own subjective value system, a relatively stable system that regulates human behavior and through which the subject values any new object or phenomenon.

In the third plane of analysis are the established and officially recognized values. This instituted system can be the result of the generalization of one of the existing subjective scales in society or of the combination of several of them. In general, certain individuals or groups that hold power are those who impose this system on the rest of the social universe in question, by making their scale of values official. In reality, all these different dimensions of values interact with each other in multiple ways. From the axiological point of view, sociologists, anthropologists and ethnologists make values the consensual result of the collective conscience of society.

Frondizi (1958) addressed the problem of the objectification and subjectivation of values, warning about the possibility that scientific practices incurred objectivism and subjectivism. Values can become motivational sources for social subjects and guide their behavior, if they are subjectively assumed by them, by their conscience. Value is not mechanically incorporated or internalized to individual subjectivity, but in a long process of active construction of the personal meaning that the subject is capable of giving to said content based on his or her history, personal resources and sociocultural context in their lives. The individual, in his or her ontogenetic trajectory, will mediate external influences.

This understanding is in line with prominent scholars in the field regarding the dynamic and contradictory nature of values in their individual subjectivation or internalization.[2] It is also important to consider that in the process of assigning value, the universal, national, group and individual histories of the subject are integrated in an inseparable synthesis. These integrations can be expressed in the unique and unrepeatable configuration that each subject has as a conception of the world.

In the process of worldview formation, the person is not only educated but can also choose a conscious and active way of understanding the world, identifying with certain scientific concepts and forming their attitude toward the real problems in society. The worldview is not only knowledge, but also an internal position of the individual, which implies meanings of what she or he has learned. Value attributions are associated with satisfying the needs of the individual, no matter the recipient of that value: objects, people, situations, norms, ideals, symbols. Personal meanings are attributed to the object in relation to the motivations of the subject. Attitudes, character traits, interests, habits, needs, motivations and ideals are structural components of the personality, like other complex formations. All these psychological senses influence the assimilation of the evaluative content as the basis for the configuration of the conception of the world and its repercussion on the regulation and self-regulation of human behavior.

This inner reality, prior to each daily act, is what constitutes the subjectivation of value from the individual angle. It is a system of judgments about good and evil, justice, happiness, love, gratitude, perseverance, moral and social content that have been developing since the early years of childhood, from the education received within the family and from teachers, and predisposes the individual to think, feel, act and behave in a predictable, consistent and stable way, as well as to understand and esteem others. That is why the individual gives meaning to life and facilitates a mature and balanced relationship with the environment, with people, events and things, providing feelings of personal harmony.

López (2005a, 2005b) considered that when analyzing its dimensions as a social phenomenon, values must be understood as "the compass of human behavior," since there are no acts of essence in man in which they are not manifested explicitly or implicitly. Values are at the top of the personality, of human spirituality, they guide the development of people, taken as individuals or as groups, toward good or evil, in all its nuances and expressions in the different spheres and contexts. Values are also part of the conception of the world; they are one of its most active elements and also essential pillars of the philosophy of the individual's life. The lack of a well-defined and internally settled value system predisposes the subject to vagueness and existential emptiness, leaving him or her at the mercy of external criteria and guidelines to discern and make decisions. It is a philosophy of life, which also needs love, friendship and the satisfaction of physiological needs. Lacking a value system can have, among other social consequences, that of leaving the person in question to develop as a selfish, nihilistic, impulsive, skeptical human being who lives out a meaningless life.

The human development of adolescents and young people refers to the achievement of the development of physical, spiritual, creative and social potentialities with full enjoyment of citizenship rights in a solidary and equitable society. Donas (2001) makes reference to the challenges to the formation of values in youth, taking into account their generalized expression in Latin American youth. Among these challenges are: loss of values, culture of consumption and consumption of culture, culture of risk, culture of pleasure, culture of the body, relations between genders, management of sexuality/genitality, among others. In his research, he compiles studies by Latin American psychologists, sociologists and anthropologists, which allowed him to address each of these challenges and their impact on the human development of adolescents and young people. Particularly relevant here is Donas' emphasis on dichotomous positions that affect the existence and subjective well-being of Latin American youths, because they are related to the sociopsychological problems of the Cuban youth studied.

In Cuba, Hitchman et al. (2012) conducted a study using a survey on the formation of values in young people who studied health technologies. The results showed that 100% of participants affirmed that we perceive a loss (crisis) of values at the moment, and that the fundamental causes are in the first place not having adequate family training (75%), and secondly, not having adequate training in school (55%). The crisis manifests through experiences of sadness, passivity, apathy, future uncertainty and a tendency to consume psychotropic drugs to alleviate some of these symptoms. The settings where these symptoms were expressed with the greatest regularity were at school and in the family. Relatedly, Amaro (2014) carried out an investigation on ethical values and anti-values perceived and expressed by university students. The results revealed: the virtues that they admire most are: sincerity and generosity; the defects they do not tolerate in others are: selfishness and lies. The values are solidarity and justice; anti-values were selfishness and double standards. The analysis of the contextualization of these values and anti-values in Cuban society serve as a reference for my research to understand the social, political, economic, cultural and educational factors that influence the formation and education of values in young Cubans.

The transformations in the Cuban socioeconomic context in the last ten years have had a particular influence on the development spaces of adolescents and young people, including and in fundamental processes such as continuity of studies, professional choice and cultural consumption.

In general, the following problems experienced by Cuban youth today are:

- The living conditions of the family can make a difference regarding the possibility of facilitating the youth's access to university.
- Hence, there is an accelerated increase in the percentage of young people employed in the non-state sector of the economy and the trend toward important changes in their composition by occupational categories. The utilitarian nature of work is reinforced, while interest in self-improvement and social contribution diminishes. (Almeyda & Bueno, 2015).
- Cultural consumption from the use of technologies. Expósito and Martínez (2015) found in their research that young university students who use mobile phones have acquired new forms of social power and new ways to organize and share information. Based on research carried out on ethics and aesthetics, some manifestations of existential attitudes have been addressed in this stage, such as: existential lack of solidarity, excessive consumerism, pragmatic-utilitarian

attitudes and existential presentism caused by the dehistoricization of projects of human life and its meaning (virtual life and real life).

In the juvenile stage, as a general trend, an individual may or may not be able to configure a project and implement it. In relation to the achievement of their goals, young people may face events, potentially crisis-generating situations; between the ages of twenty and twenty-five we find delimitations of projects associated with marriage, the completion of studies and the beginning of working life. Others have already reached such achievements. Members of this youth sub-group as defined by age vary in their courses of development, and some are trapped in crises, contradictions, conflicts and frustrations.

Such is the case of those young people who have experienced existential crisis. They complain of living a meaningless life, an emptiness permeated by boredom, apathy, psychic and physical fatigue. Pessimism and a lack of initiative immobilize them in making decisions. As an adaptation mechanism, conformity usually appears as an apparent relief, passivity simulating peace, submission masked by a supposed obedience. Sometimes they manifest depersonalization: not knowing at times who they are and frequent dissociations in spatiality and temporality.

It is common to recognize in them low self-esteem, insecurity, dependency and a poverty of personal resources to restructure the field of action when they face conflicts and frustrations. Existential crisis is a problem that affects young people from all latitudes and is a recurring symptom in psychological and psychiatric assistance. Hence, multiple investigations can be found recommending alternatives for its intervention. For García (2004; as cited in Moreno, 2013), young people need vital horizons that carry meaning, that provide them with resources to answer the many questions that may appear about their existence. As such, educational action should favor answers to the questions posed by youth to stimulate their potential to find meaning in life. The loss of this vitality is the peculiar symptom of the existential crisis.

For García (2004; as cited in Moreno, 2013):

> The meaning of life is a typically human question about why and for what, where of existence. It is a question of all times and places, which in moments of crisis erupts with more virulence. Neither apathy nor lack of hope can put an end to questions about meaning. These questions pop up most strongly where the experience of nonsense is deepest. Never

> completely dampened, the question of meaning becomes more urgent in crisis situations. (p. 33)

Frankl (1988), psychiatrist and representative of existentialism, considered the meaning of life as the principle of morality, which guides the decisions that each person makes in a situation directing what actions to take because they are good or which to stop because they are bad or do not produce the desired good. Thus the construction of the meaning of life is carried out through the realization of the values that are discovered as possibilities of each situation. For this, specific circumstances are not required, but an adequate education of moral conscience insofar as it is capable of opening itself to transcendence and allowing itself to be questioned by the horizon of values that it presents. Frankl defended the criterion of promoting transdisciplinary practices to intervene in the problems that affect individuals in their biopsychosocial and spiritual integrity. For this reason, he emphasized the philosophical, psychological, sociological and anthropological bases of his study on the meaning of life.

For Frankl (1988), it is not enough for human beings to live solely to achieve biological, psychic and social balance, but they need something more; they harbor within themselves the will to do something full of meaning, to strive and fight for a goal or mission. An individual lives his or her existence to the fullest insofar as he or she is oriented toward something or someone that transcends themselves and that represents a value, an ideal, a project loaded with meaning. However, sometimes the search for an altruistic or transcendent ideology is hampered by attitudes that can damage the freedom and responsibility offered by its existence. Among them are:

- Provisional attitude toward life: it implies living from day to day due to the lack of a personal and social project.
- Fatalistic attitude toward life: considering that it is not possible to take one's own destiny in hand, because it is determined by external or internal factors and forces.
- Collectivist thinking: wanting to go unnoticed, because it is scary to assume personal responsibility, giving up one's autonomy as a person.

- Fanaticism: renouncing one's own ideas and one's conscience, without judging, for the security they bring, the ideas of a leader, a group, a hero, an organization, etc.

In my research, different manifestations of these attitudes were observed and it was striking how, faced with the experience of existential crisis, some young people could not bear the psychological pain and protected themselves through behaviors that produced fantastic images about reality. In extreme cases, somatizations occured as a mechanism to divert the harmful load of emotions into the body. Another outlet was the incorporation to a social practice in which they were able to sublimate the frustrations that generate crises, despite moving abruptly from one worldview to another. This revealed itself as a tendency toward execution, trial and error, mediated by suggestion, impulsiveness, emotional debauchery and fear. This emotion can generate a paralyzing and alienating response, especially in cases where youth do not know where to seek help.

The impossibility of satisfying needs, as well as the slowdown in encountering new objects of achievement, can lead some people to isolate themselves, to invent a "comfort zone" as a way to avoid obstacles and challenges for which they do not feel prepared. Others, through projection, build idols, fetishes, choose phenomena from reality to vent their anger through hypercriticism. Faced with existential crisis, addictions to objects, symbols, idols can be configured. Furthermore, the fear of death and the complaint of "lacking energy" are recurring signs. The behavioral manifestations described above are signs of the so-called human alienation.

The studies carried out by the humanist Erick Fromm (1958) on Karl Marx's concept of the individual (man) made it possible to understand the aforementioned signs and symptoms beyond their empirical expression. Marx argued that the concept of the active, productive man, who captures and embraces the objective world with his own faculties, cannot be fully understood without the concept of the negation of productivity: alienation. Fromm, referring to the way in which Marx characterized alienation, expressed that it leads to the perversion of all values. By making the economy and its values - profit, work, savings and sobriety - the supreme goal in life, man does not develop moral values, the wealth of a good conscience, virtue, etc. Marx wondered: how can I be virtuous if I am not alive, and how can I have a good conscience if I am not aware of anything? In alienation, each sphere of life - economic and moral -

is independent of the other, each is concentrated in a specific sphere of alienated activity and is itself alienated in relation to the other.[3]

In close connection with the ideas previously exposed are those derived from Gustavo Berti's (2012) research, in which he warns about the diversity of recurrent symptoms in young people: anxiety disorders, panic disorders, eating disorders such as anorexia and bulimia, and disorders associated with spatiality with severe sensorial-perceptual alterations. According to Berti, each of these manifestations has sociogenic causes: existential crisis, which he considers as a difficulty to accept the flow of life. Those people who are too attached to order, extremely responsible, very resistant to existential changes and very rigid in general, people who prefer to dwell in habit at all costs become susceptible to it. As such, a therapeutic approach is necessary to help the individual conceive of new ways of being in this world.

Moreno (2013), when studying university students with depression, anxiety and obsession with death, refers to the need to promote a comprehensive education in them, so that they are linked with new styles of learning to live in "this world" to find other meanings. It is urgent to evaluate the belief systems and limiting valuations of young people around the conflictive areas of their lives, which become potentialities of existential crisis. Faced with the impossibility of making decisions, an individual becomes more insecure, dissociated and sometimes desperate. When the concepts, evaluations and judgments constructed do not allow resizing the conflictive and frustrating situation, it is sometimes necessary to unlearn and appropriate new ideas and information to understand what is happening.

Understanding challenges and situations in life can also be hampered by the existence of limiting conceptions and beliefs. Sometimes this lead to dichotomous fragmentation of life and the perception of the individual's very existence. Fromm (1959) studied the relationship between having and being and the repercussions that their dichotomization can have. According to him, existential dichotomies are usually contradictions originating from human attributes; unsolved conflicts, such as wishing for immortality and knowing that we must die; wanting perfection, but having to live with imperfection. Frankl (1988) stated that there are different planes of existence: biological, psychological, social and spiritual, all interrelated. Despite this, there are people with neurotic disorders who live in fragmentation. They weigh the biological and the social and neglect their psychological and spiritual existence. These are the individuals focused on having rather than being. On the other hand, subjects can be identified who focus only on the psychological and neglect other planes.

In my research, I identified many over-generalized beliefs whose essence is reductionist and linear, rather than dialectical. Ellis (1974) identified certain common thinking errors, including: all-or-nothing thoughts; over-generalization; interpretation instead of description; correlation confused with causality; and unspoken assumptions or beliefs. The identification of beliefs and thoughts such as these are frequently identified in psychological and psychiatric assistance. The readjustment of thought through its operations of analysis, synthesis, comparison, generalization and abstraction can facilitate a change of beliefs. In this way, crisis can be experienced as a means to grow and develop as a personality. When a subject becomes aware of his or her life through healthy beliefs, he or she reaches a state of adjustment and balance that favors all its dimensions.

The study of the latent, the implicit, the symbolic, is another useful behavioral manifestation to study the existential crisis in any individual. Psychologists must dynamically study human subjectivity from the interaction of the conscious and the unconscious. Over the course of my research, I wondered if the problems of the young people evaluated could transcend the individual level, and perhaps express themselves, implicitly, symbolically, latent in other social groups. To facilitate this analysis, I took the theory of symbolic interactionism of George Herbert Mead (1938) was taken into account. Some of its principles stimulated reflections on the significance of existential crisis at a group, institutional and perhaps macrosocial level For me, it was important to stimulate reflection and personal elaboration of my research participants around the active role that they have in the assimilation and appropriation of the meanings, senses and symbols born of the interaction with their reality. At the same time, I encouraged them to consider the responsibility and protagonism they have before the possibility of influencing the introduction of modifications and alternatives, due to their ability to interact with themselves and with various groups.

Correspondingly with this, I identified the need emerged to offer young people a dialectical conception that allows them to understand the essence of the phenomena of their existence, without violating their worldview. This dialectical vision allows us to value the phenomena and processes of life in motion, in transformation, in advances, in setbacks, in contradictions, in their differences, antagonisms, in their diversity and unity. Such an approach approximates the application of the dialectical relationship of the philosophical categories: cause-effect; essence and phenomenon; necessity and chance; content and form; possibility and reality; the abstract and the concrete; the historical and the logical; the general, the particular and the singular.

Each category reflects an aspect of the objective world and all of them conventionally encompass, in an approximate form, the objective, universal regularity of nature in eternal movement and development. The categories constitute a complete system and can only be understood as elements of a certain system. Its implementation in the field of clinical psychology can help to understand the contradictory relationships between the processes of the same subjective level and also those that correspond to another. An example of this is the understanding of the sense of self, the functioning of the personality. It is considered necessary to instruct and educate an individual who presents existential crisis in the idea that his or her life and that of others are not a cause or consequence of all or nothing.

Understanding the course of individual development or life history reveals the non-linear relationships between multiple causes and their effects; between what is experienced as necessary and as coincidental. The realization of life goals or projects is traversed by the real and the possible, the historical and the logical, the essential and the phenomenal. The meaning of life is a content of the personality that allows the subject to reveal its essence and this enables the phenomenal expression of the integral parts of the personological system. The relationship of the general, the particular and the singular reveals the essence of the principle of the determinism of the psychic in all its levels of expression.

I agree with D'Angelo (1998) that the meaning of personal life lacks real content if it is restricted to the exclusively individual existential sphere. The individual is not encapsulated in his or her own subjectivity. Instead, his or her subjectivity is inevitably a social as well as a personal construction. The phenomenon of existential crisis in young people must be evaluated and intervened in its complexity, diversity of expression, in its multi-determination and in the possibilities of being reoriented toward human development and psychological well-being.

The various axiological and sociological evaluations carried out on existential crisis in youth offer a deeper vision of possible diagnoses and psychological interventions. If these processes are analyzed only from the clinical aspect of Psychology and Psychiatry, the understanding of the structure and integrative functioning of the human being can be fragmented. As such, I propose that diagnosis and intervention be based on the intersection between Psychology, Axiology, Sociology and Philosophy.

Notes

1. For more, see Febles (1999) and González (2000).
2. See Cristóbal and Domínguez (2003), Domínguez (2003, 2007), Domínguez et al. (2014), Fernández (2002; 2005), and Fernández-Ballesteros (2005).
3. See also Marx (1975) and Fromm (1959).

Bibliography

Agulló, E., & Ovejero, A. (Eds.). (2001). *Trabajo, individuo y sociedad. Perspectivas psicosociológicas sobre el futuro del trabajo.* Pirámide.

Almeyda, A., & Bueno, G. (2015). Elecciones profesionales de jóvenes cubanos en un context de cambio social. *Revista Estudios Sobre La Juventud, 18*, 45–50.

Amaro, M. C. (2014). Una aproximación a los valores éticos consensuados por la sociedad cubana. *Educación Médica Superior, 28*(1), 35–49.

Berti, G. (2012). Trastornos de la espacialidad. Crisis existenciales en la modernidad líquida. *Revista de la Facultad de Psicología y Humanidades, 20*(2), 9–21.

Comas, D., Aguinaga, J., Orizo, F. A., Espinosa, A., & Ochaita, E. (Eds.). (2003). *Jóvenes y estilos de vida. Valores y riesgos en los jóvenes urbanos.* Injuve.

Cristóbal, D., & Domínguez, M. (2003). *Las investigaciones sobre la juventud en Cuba.* Boletín Academia (Colegio de Ciencias Sociales Universidad de La Habana).

D'Angelo, O. (1998). Formación para el desarrollo de proyectos de vida reflexivos y creativos en los campos social y profesional. *Revista Crecemos Internacional, 2*, 54–67.

Domínguez, L. (2003). Edad juvenil. In L. Domínguez (Ed.), *Psicología del desarrollo adolescencia y juventud. Selección de lecturas* (pp. 471–477). Editorial Universitaria Félix Varela.

Domínguez, L. (2007). *Psicología del desarrollo [Versión electrónica].* Editorial Universitaria Félix Varela.

Domínguez, M. I., Rego, I., & Castilla, C. (2014). *Socialización de adolescentes y jóvenes. Retos y oportunidades para la sociedad cubana actual*. Editorial de Ciencias Sociales.

Donas, S. (Ed.). (2001). *Adolescencia y juventud en América Latina*. Libro Universitario Regional.

Ellis, A. (1974). Rational-emotive theory. In A. Burton (Ed.), *Operational theories of personality* (pp. 308–344). Brunner/Mazel.

Expósito, E., & Martínez, A. C. (2015). Consumos culturales. Acercamientos teóricos y empíricos a partir de la experiencia de los jóvenes universitarios del oriente cubano. *Revista Estudios Sobre La Juventud, 18*, 35–45.

Fabelo Corzo, J.R. (1989). Práctica, conocimiento y valoración. Editorial de Ciencias Sociales.

Fabelo Corzo, J. R. (2003). *Los valores y sus desafíos actuales* (2nd ed.). Editorial José Martí.

Febles, M. (1999). La orientación psicológica desde el enfoque histórico-cultural Consideraciones generales. *Revista Cubana De Psicología, 16*(3), 211–213.

Fernández, L. (2002). *Personalidad y Relaciones de Pareja*. Editorial Universitaria Félix Varela.

Fernández, L. (Ed.). (2005). *Pensando en la Personalidad* (Vol. 1). Editorial Universitaria Félix Varela.

Fernández-Ballesteros, R. (2005). *Evaluación Psicológica. Conceptos, Métodos y Estudio de Caso*. Editorial Pirámide.

Frankl, V. (1980). *Ante el vacío existencial*. Herder.

Frankl, V. (1988). *La voluntad de sentido*. Herder.

Fromm, E. (1958). *Marx y su concepto del hombre*. Fondo de Cultura Económica.

Fromm, E. (1959). Values, psychology, and human existence. In A. H. Maslow (Ed.), *New knowledge in human values* (pp. 151–164). Harper and Row.

Frondizi, R. (1958). *¿Qué son los valores? Introducción a la axiología*. Fondo de Cultura Económica.

García, J. (2004). *El sentido de la vida: una pregunta necesaria*. Universidad Pontificia de Salamanca.

González, F. (1998). Los valores y su significación en el desarrollo de la persona. *Temas, 15*, 4–10.

González, V. (2000). La educación de valores en el currículum universitario. Un enfoque psicopedagógico para su estudio. *Educación Médica Superior, 14*(1), 74–82.

Hitchman, D., Machado, I., & Panol, M. (2012). La formación de valores de la juventud de nuestros días. *Revista Cubana De Higiene y Epidemiología, 50*(3), 427–437.

López, B. (2005a). *El saber ético de ayer a hoy*. Editorial Universitaria Félix Varela.

López, B. (2005b). La subjetivación de los valores. El papel de la regulación moral en este proceso. In L. Fernández (Ed.), *Pensando en la personalidad* (Vol. 1). Editorial Universitaria Félix Varela.

Marx, C. (1975). *Contribución a la crítica de la economía política*. Editorial de Ciencias Sociales.

Mead, G. H. (1938). *Persona, espíritu y sociedad*. Paidós.

Moral, M., & Ovejero, A. (2004). Jóvenes, globalización y postmodernidad: Crisis de la adolescencia social en una sociedad adolescente en crisis. *Papeles Del Psicólogo, 87*, 72–79.

Moreno, M. V. (2013). *Sentido de la vida y afectividad negativa* (ansiedad, depresión y obsesión por la muerte) en universitarios (unpublished doctoral thesis). Universidad de Extremadura, Spain.

Urra, J. (2004). Prólogo. In J. M. Fernández Millán & G. Buela-Casal (Eds.), *Manual para padres desesperados con hijos adolescentes* (pp. 11–16). Pirámide.

The manufacturer's authorised representative in the EU is Springer Nature Customer Service Centre GmbH, Europaplatz 3, 69115 Heidelberg, Germany. If you have any concerns regarding our products, please contact ProductSafety@springernature.com

Printed and bound by CPI Group (UK) Ltd, Croydon, CR0 4YY
30/09/2026
02225475-0017